I am grateful to god for everythand i believe that the meaning of life is to make sense other . M . E. you are the meaning of my life.

Marcos Fernandes

2024

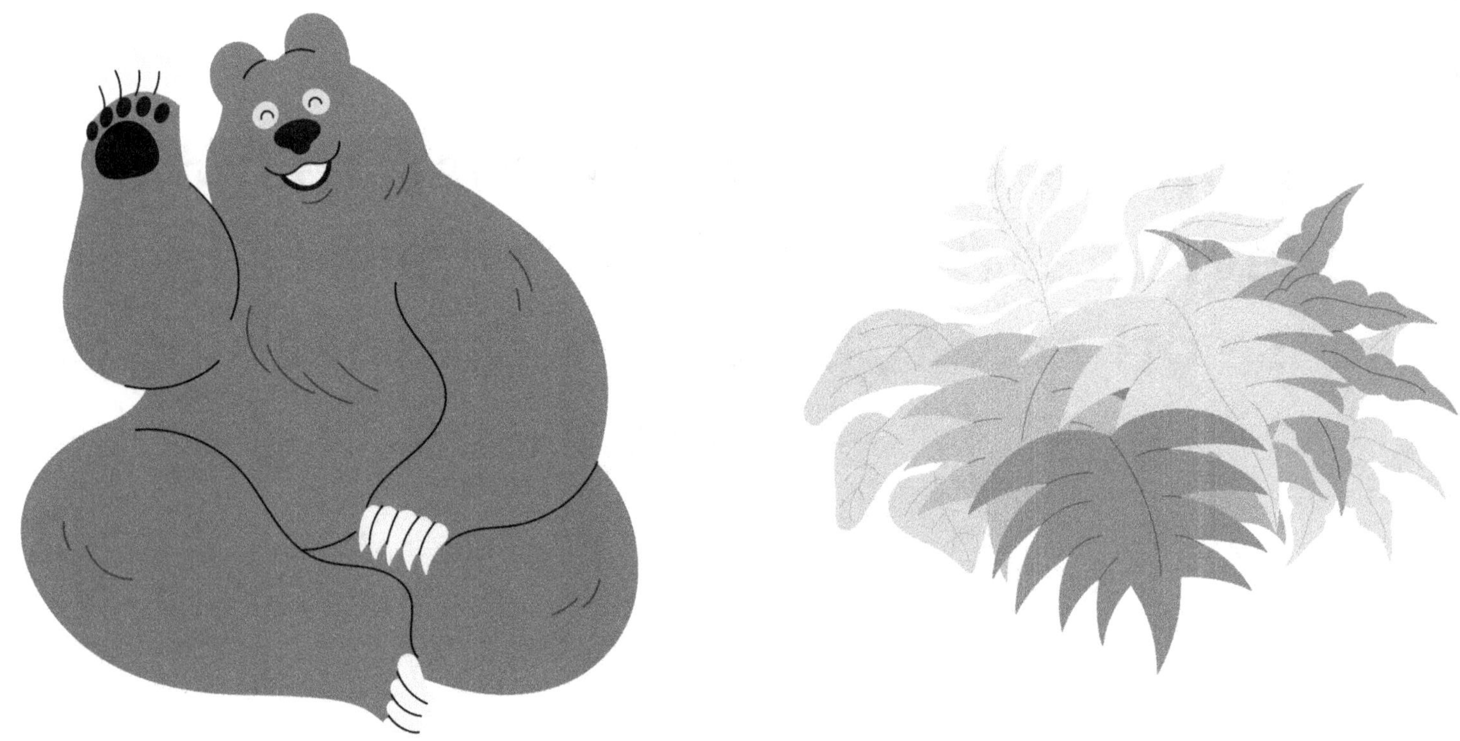

This book belongs to:

____

M.D.S.F©

**Marcos Fernandes
Publications**

Test Color Page

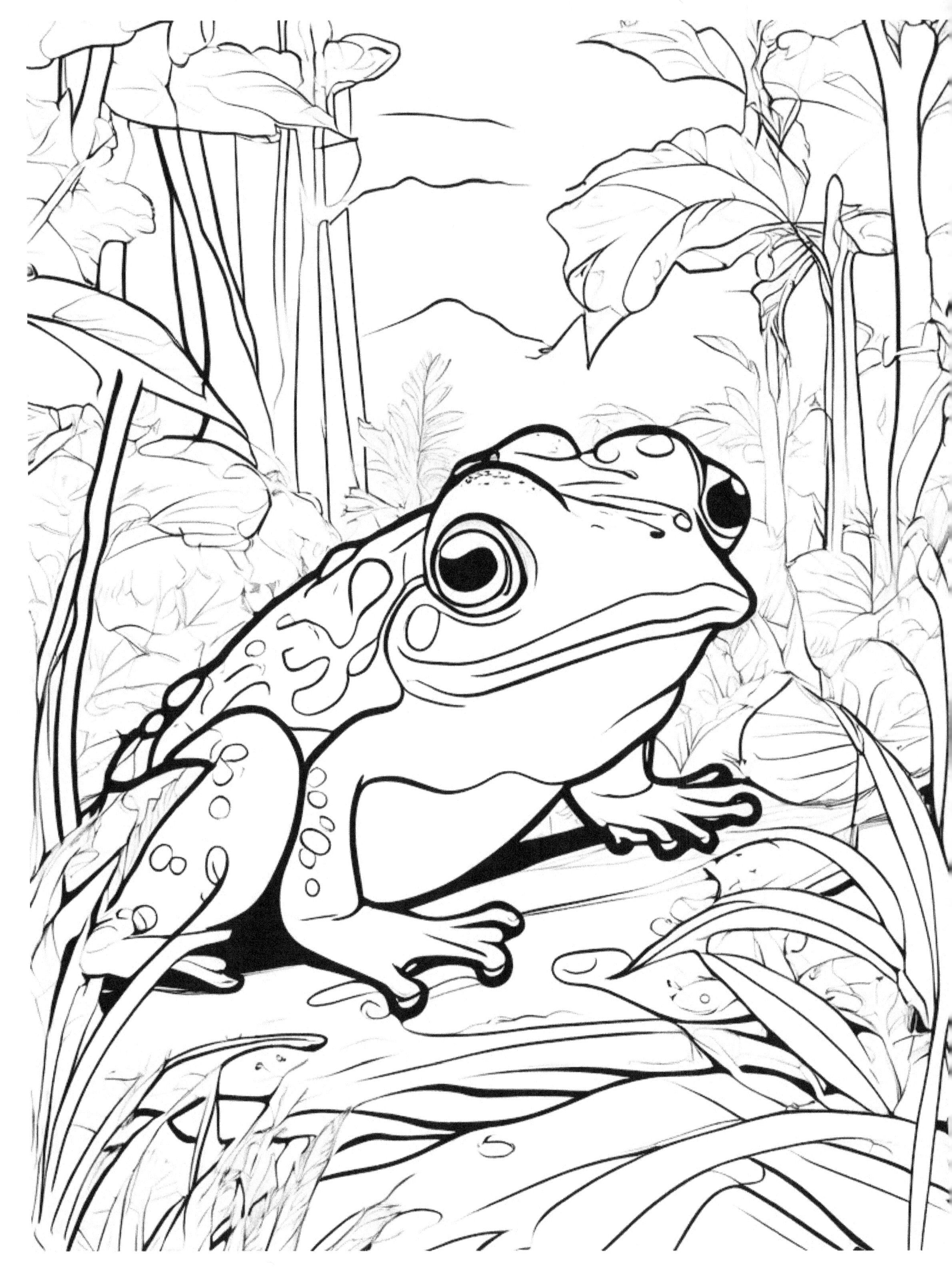

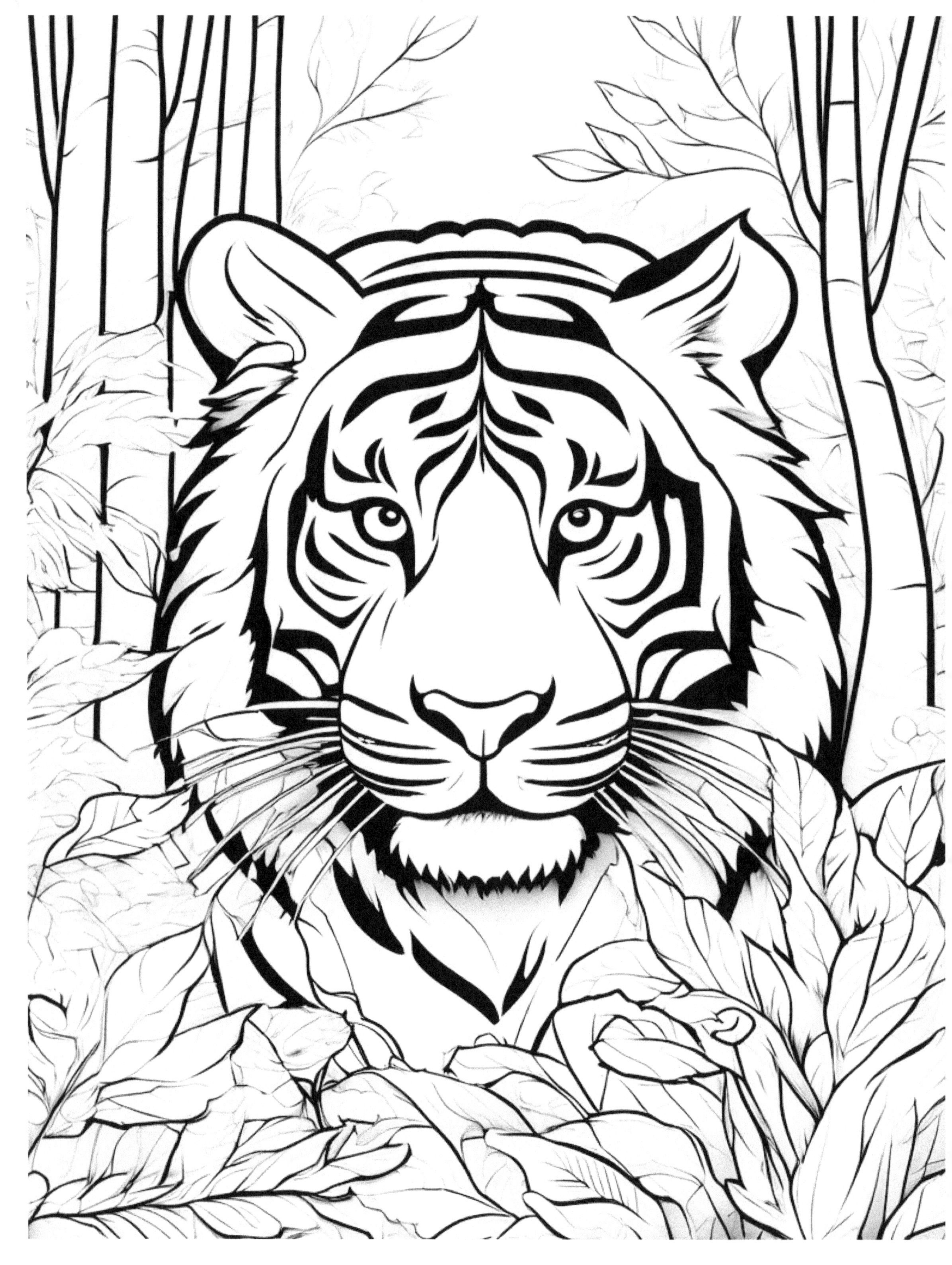

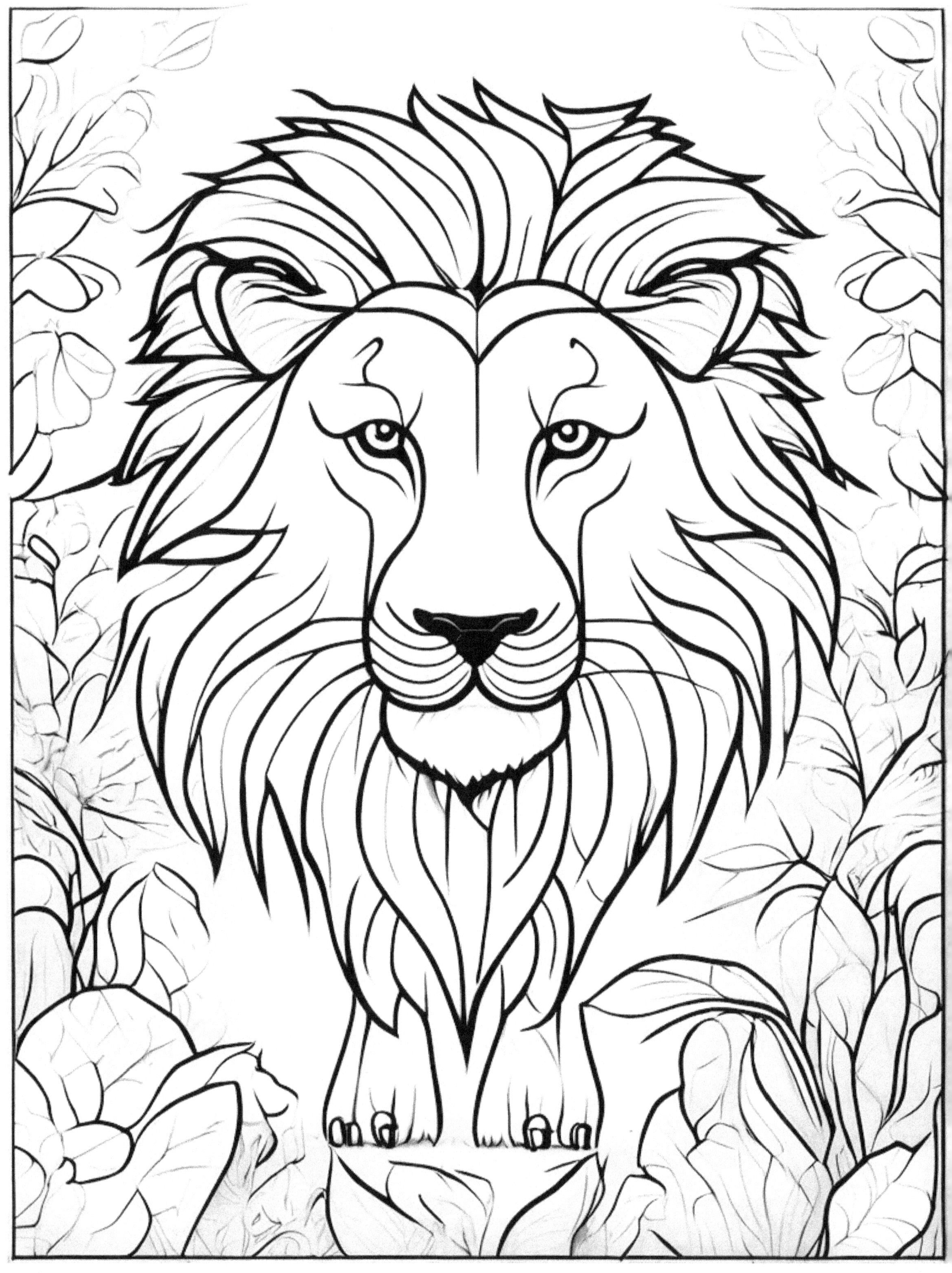

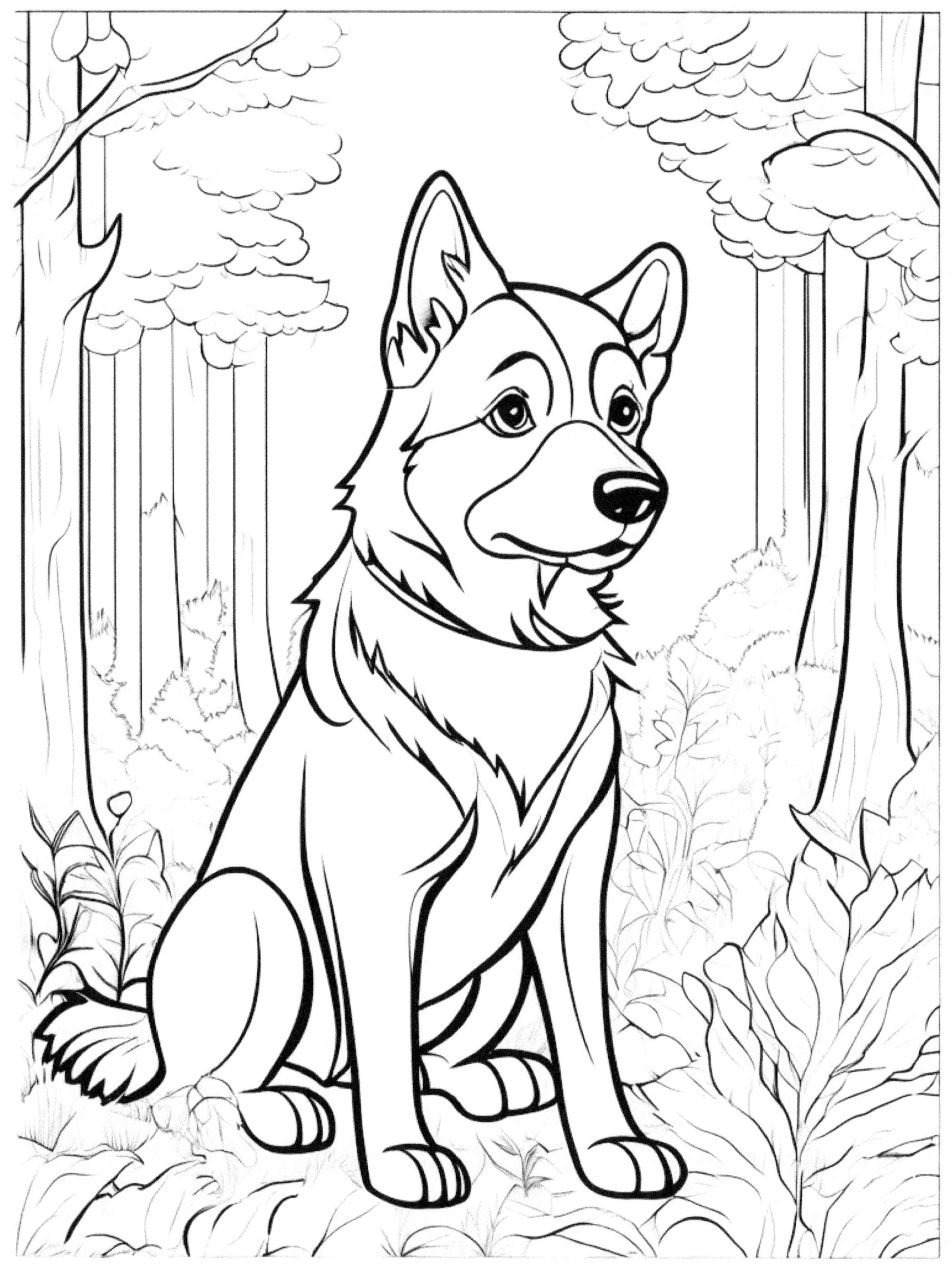

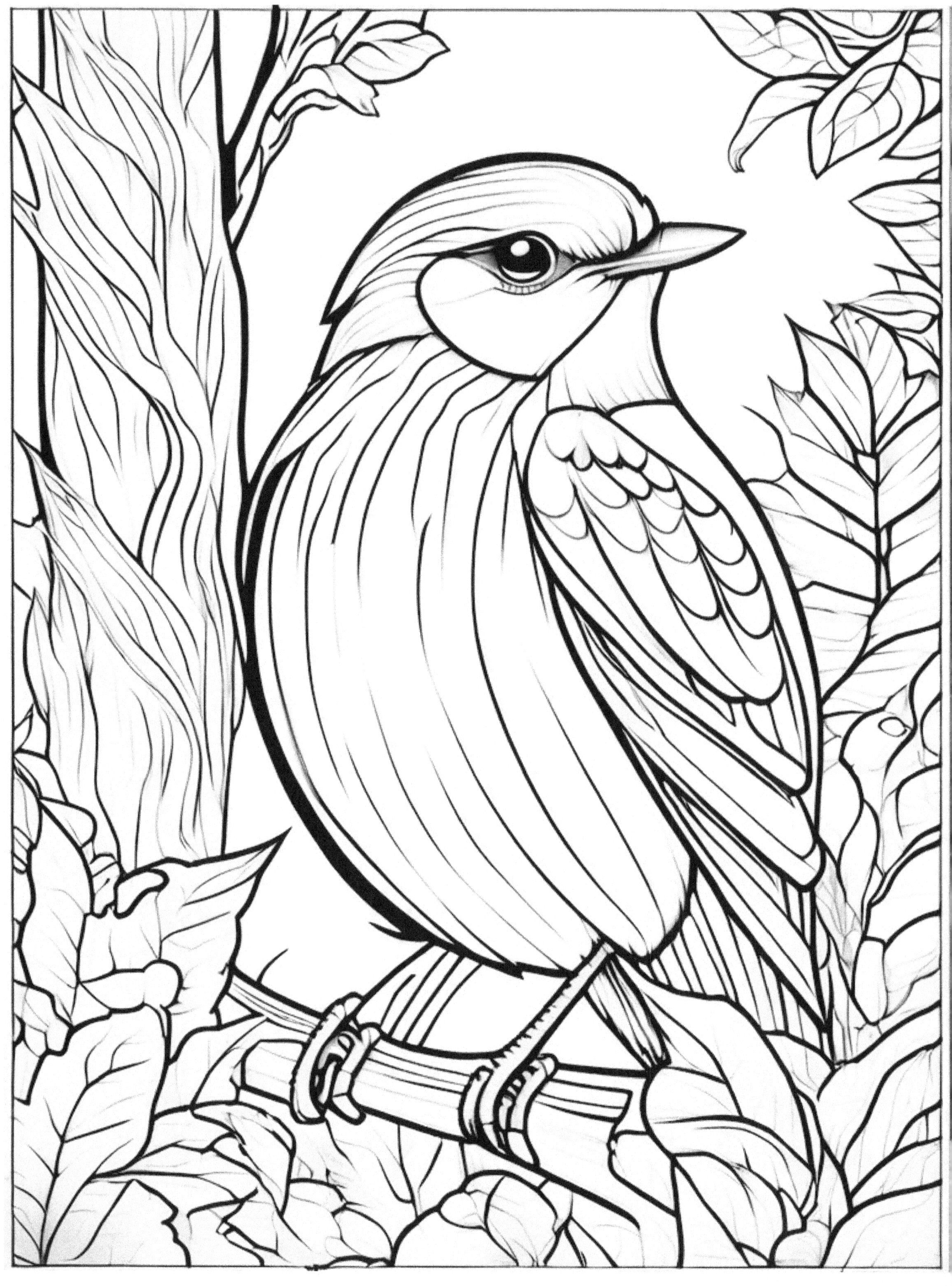

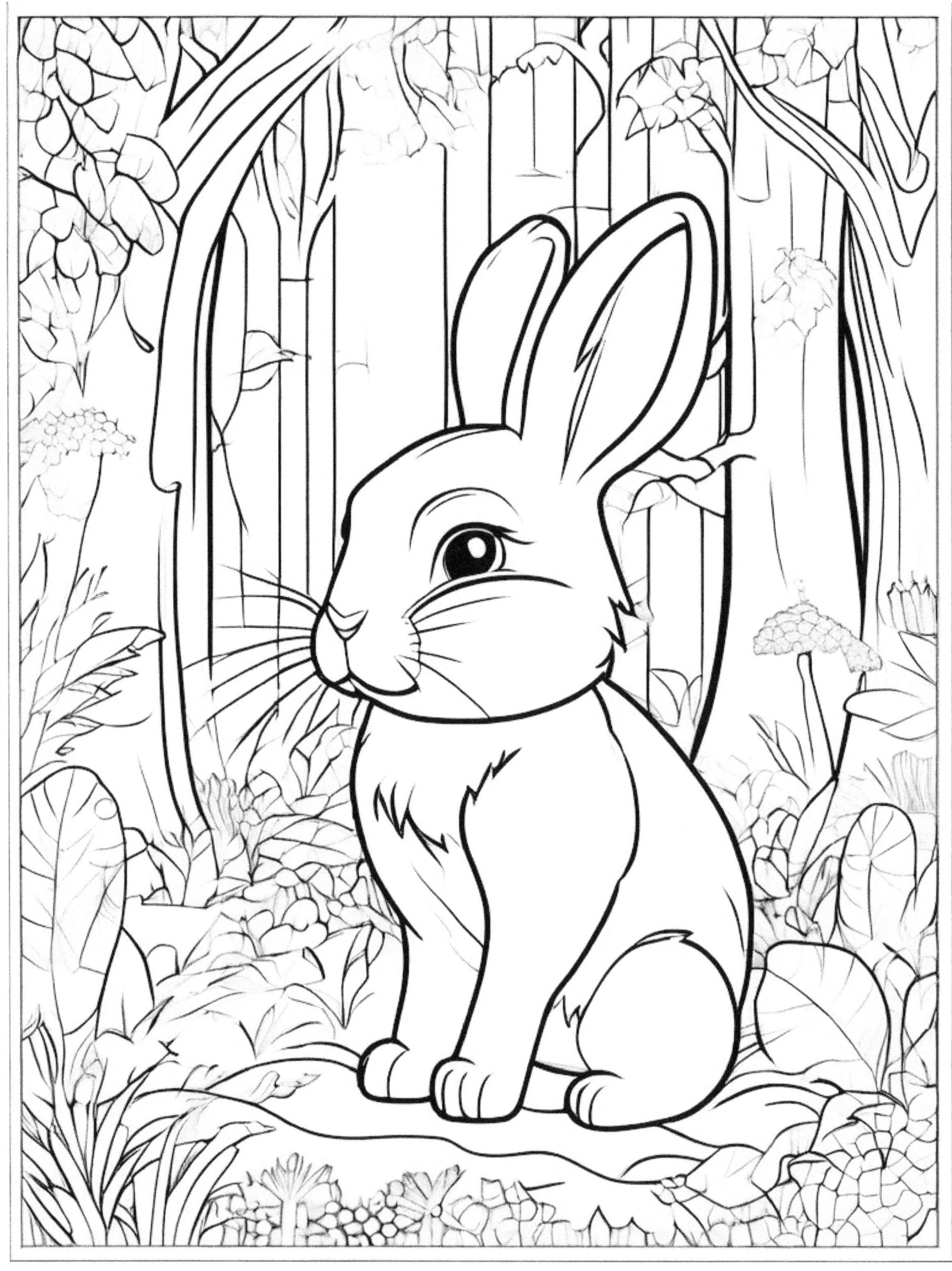

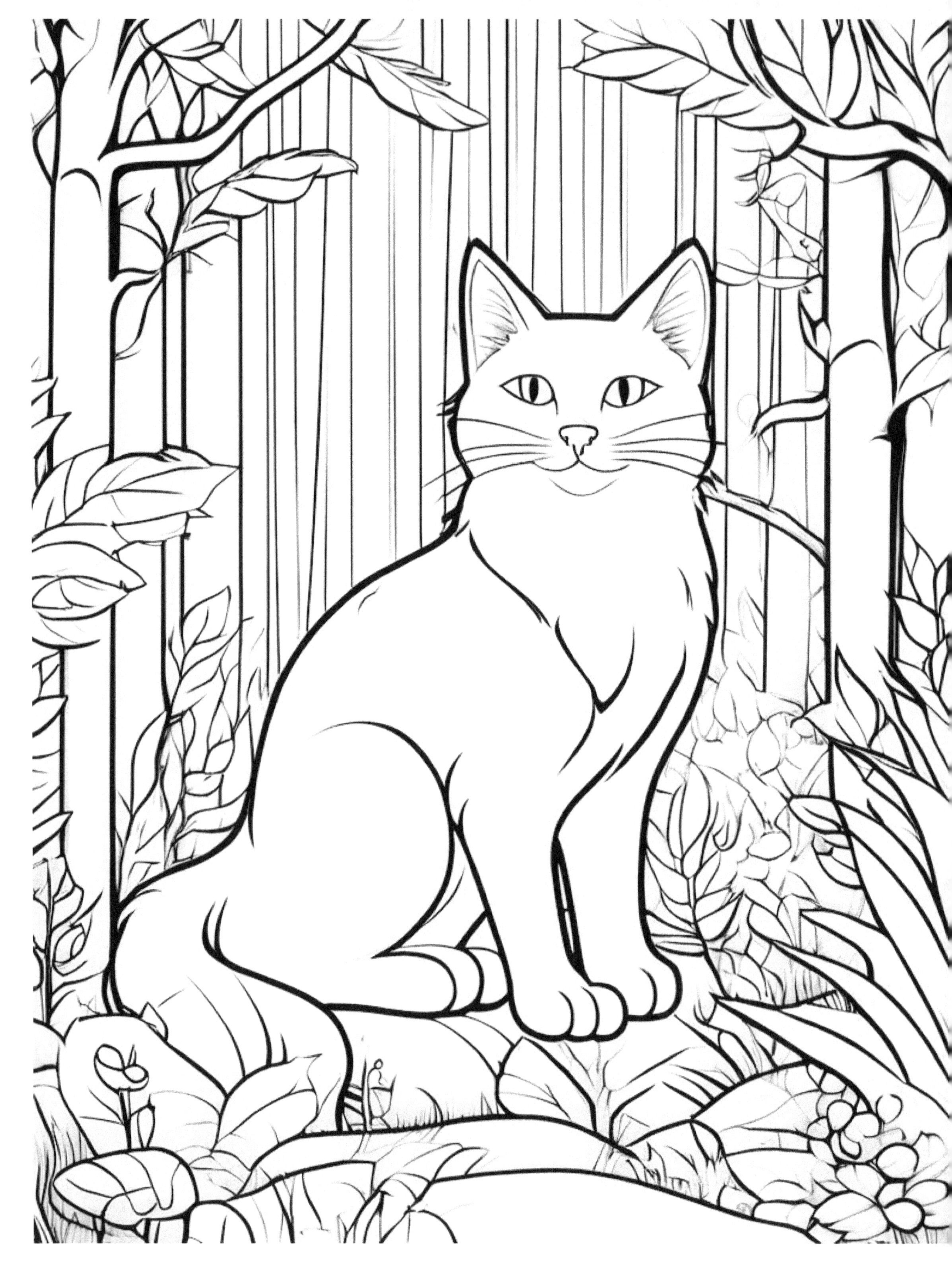

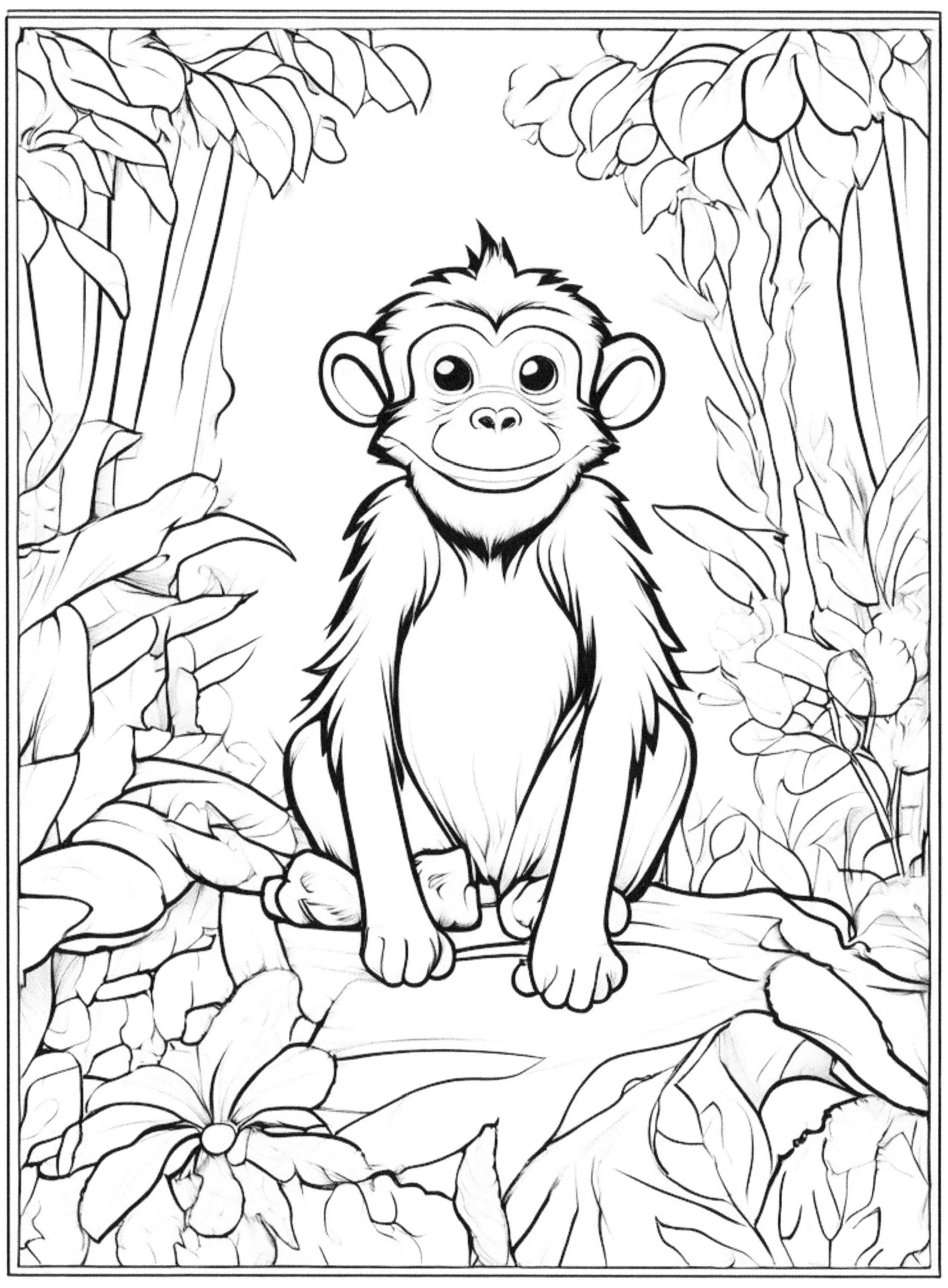

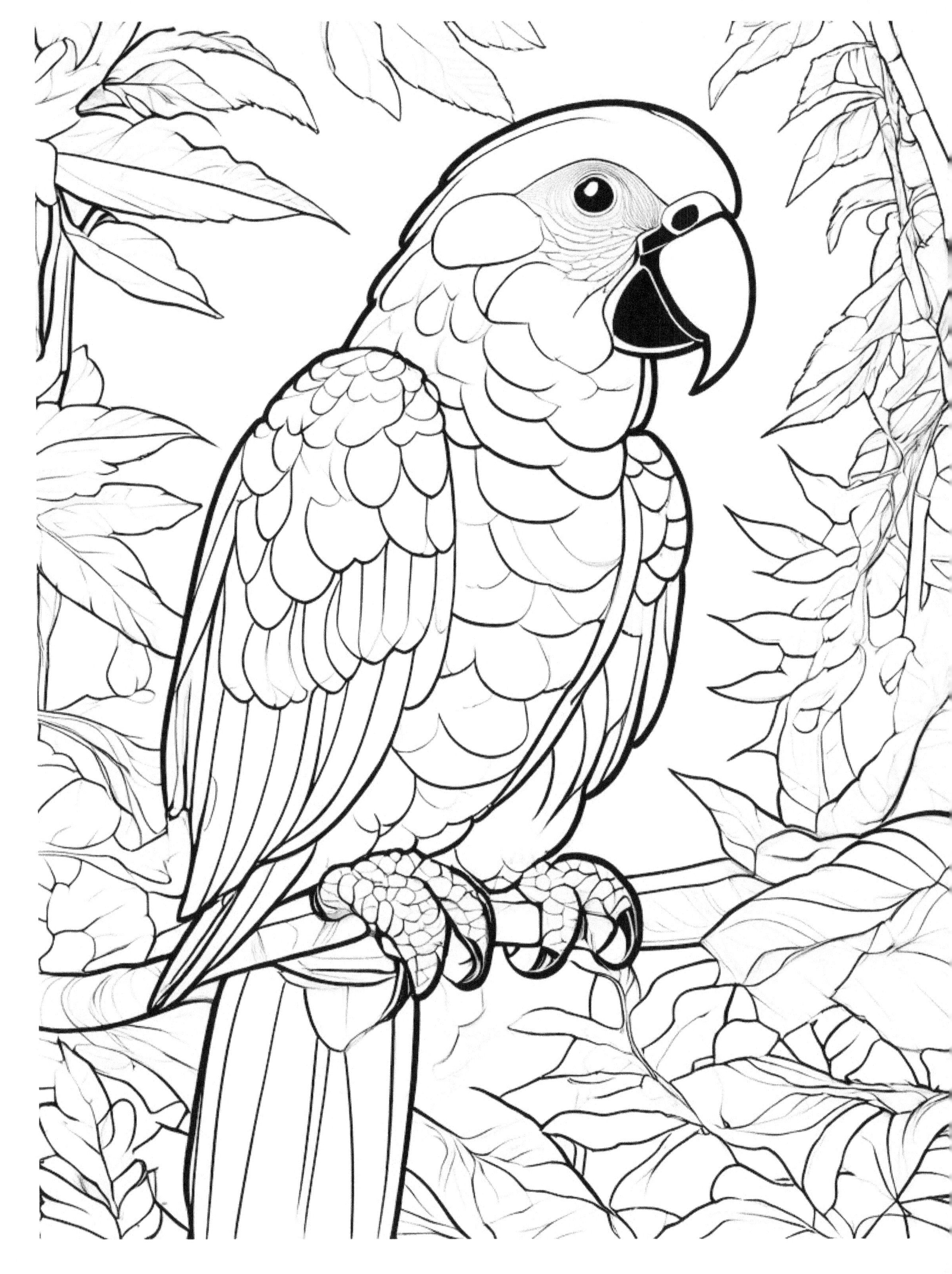

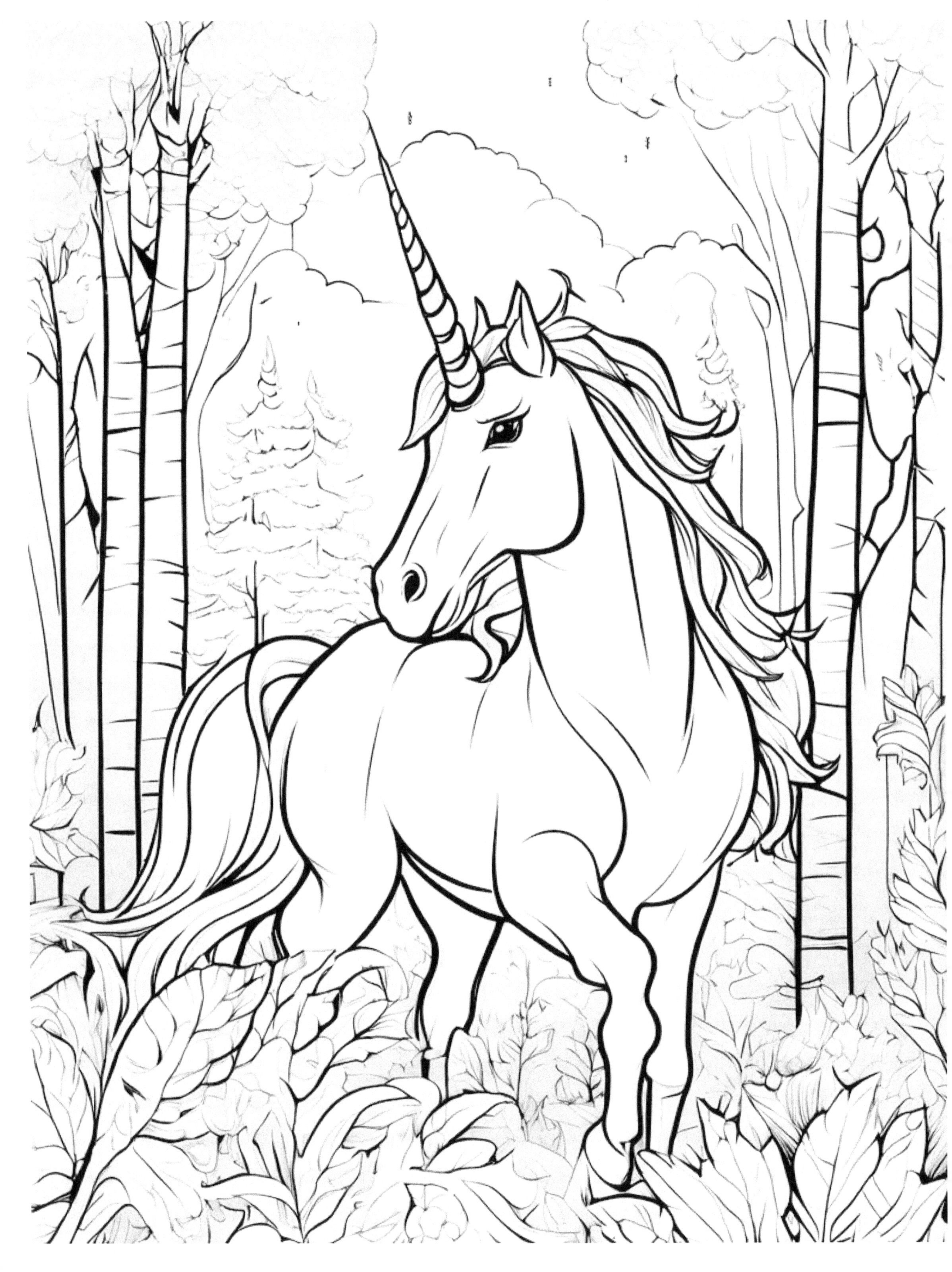

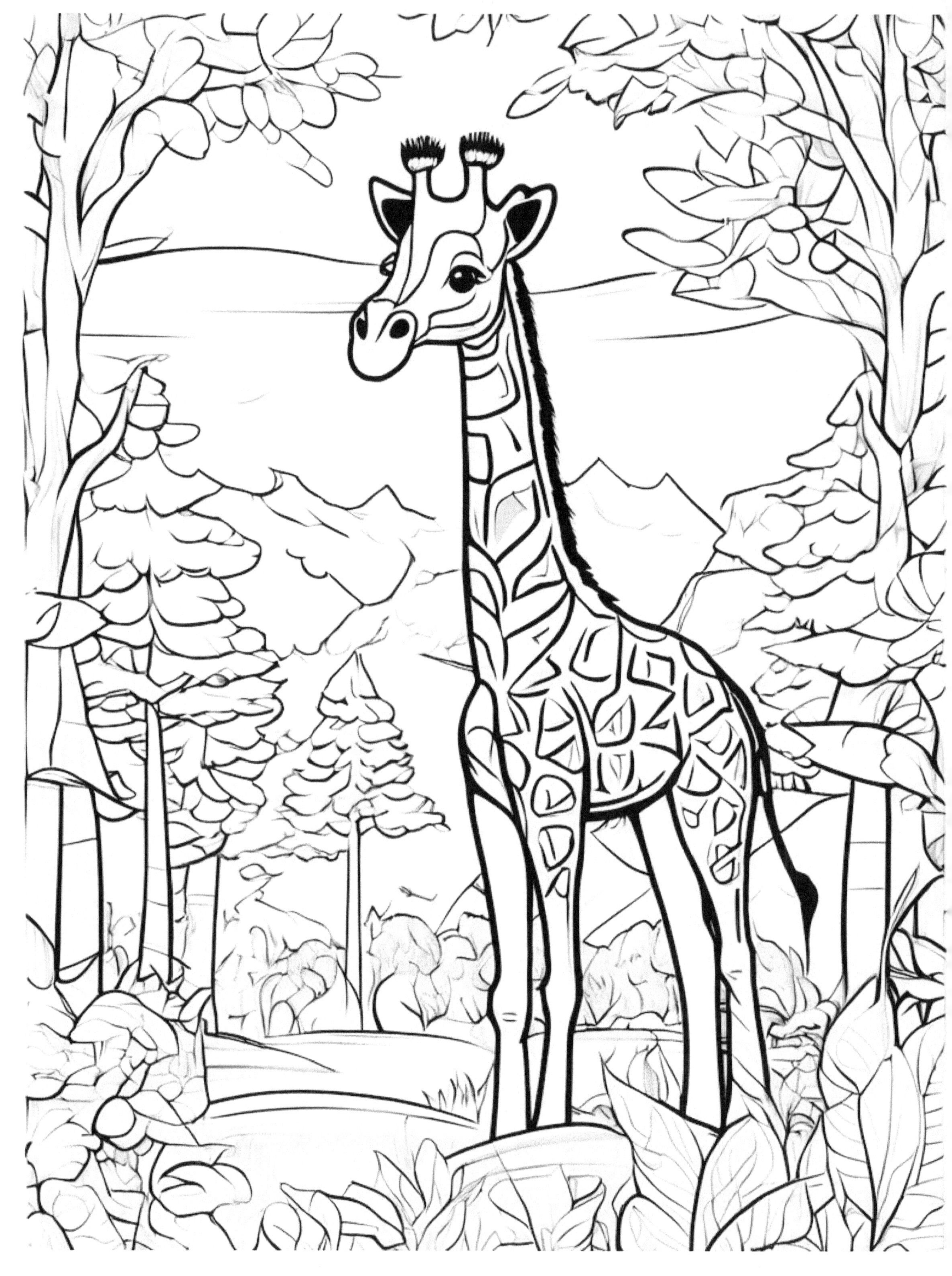

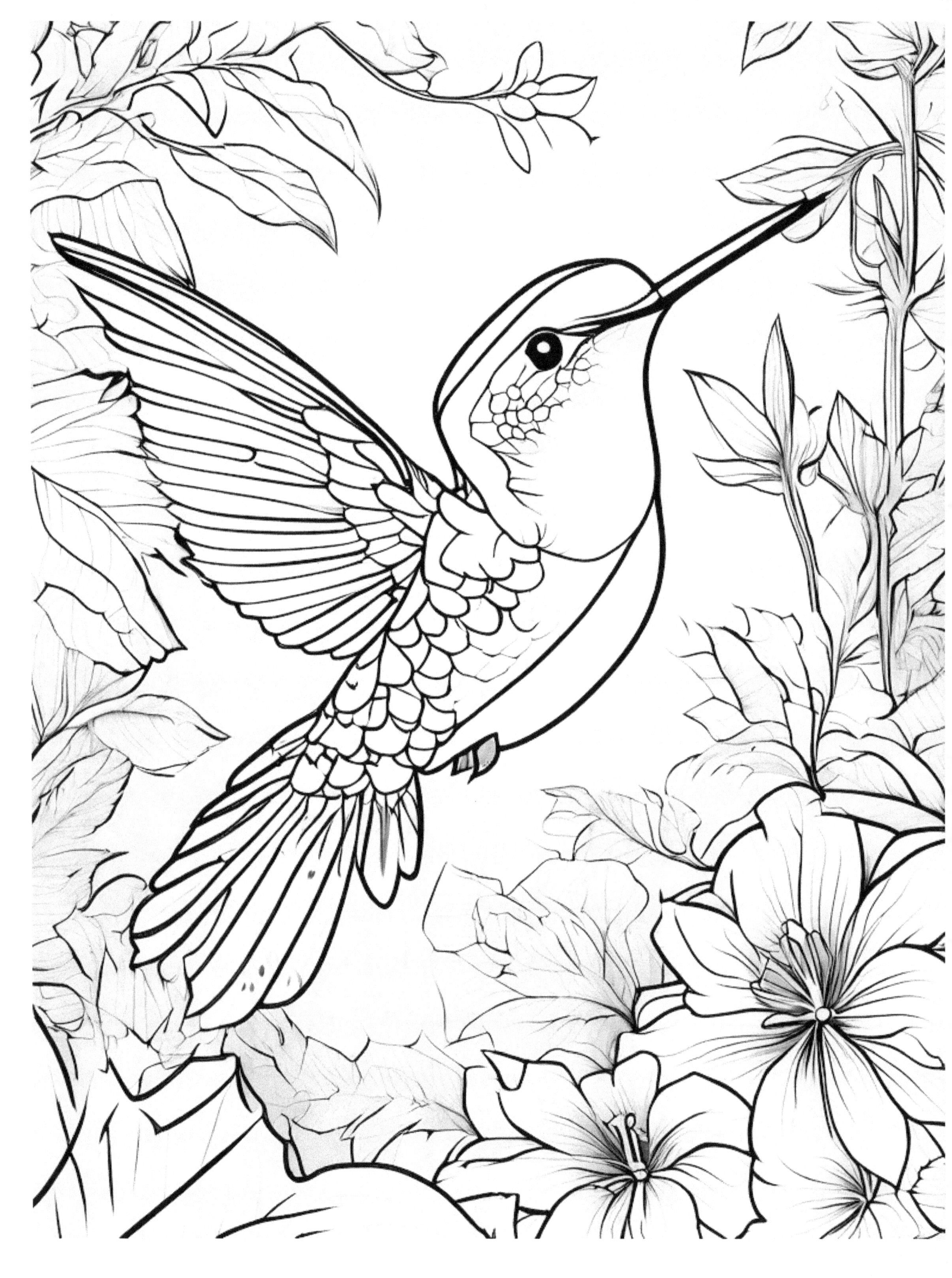

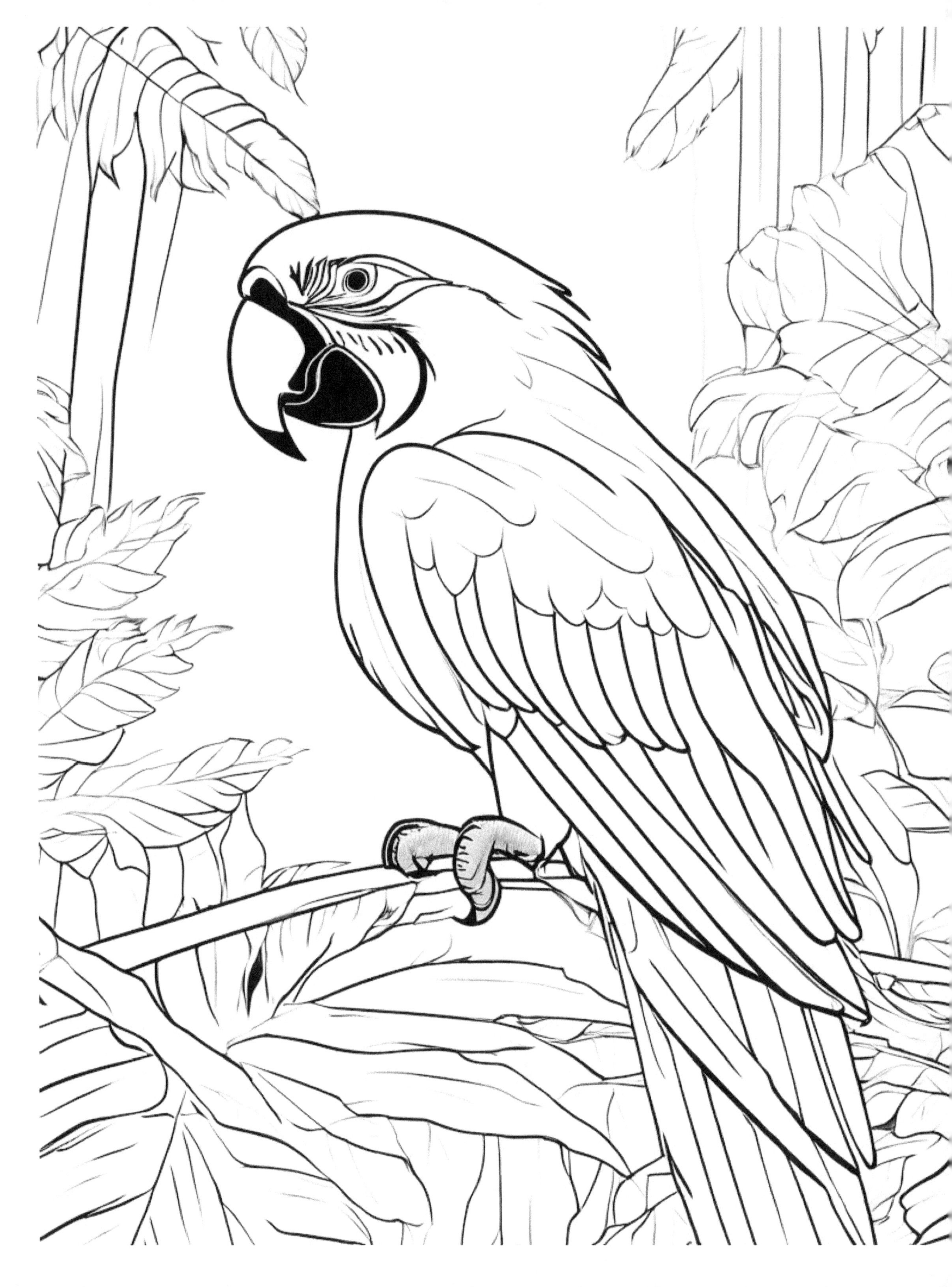

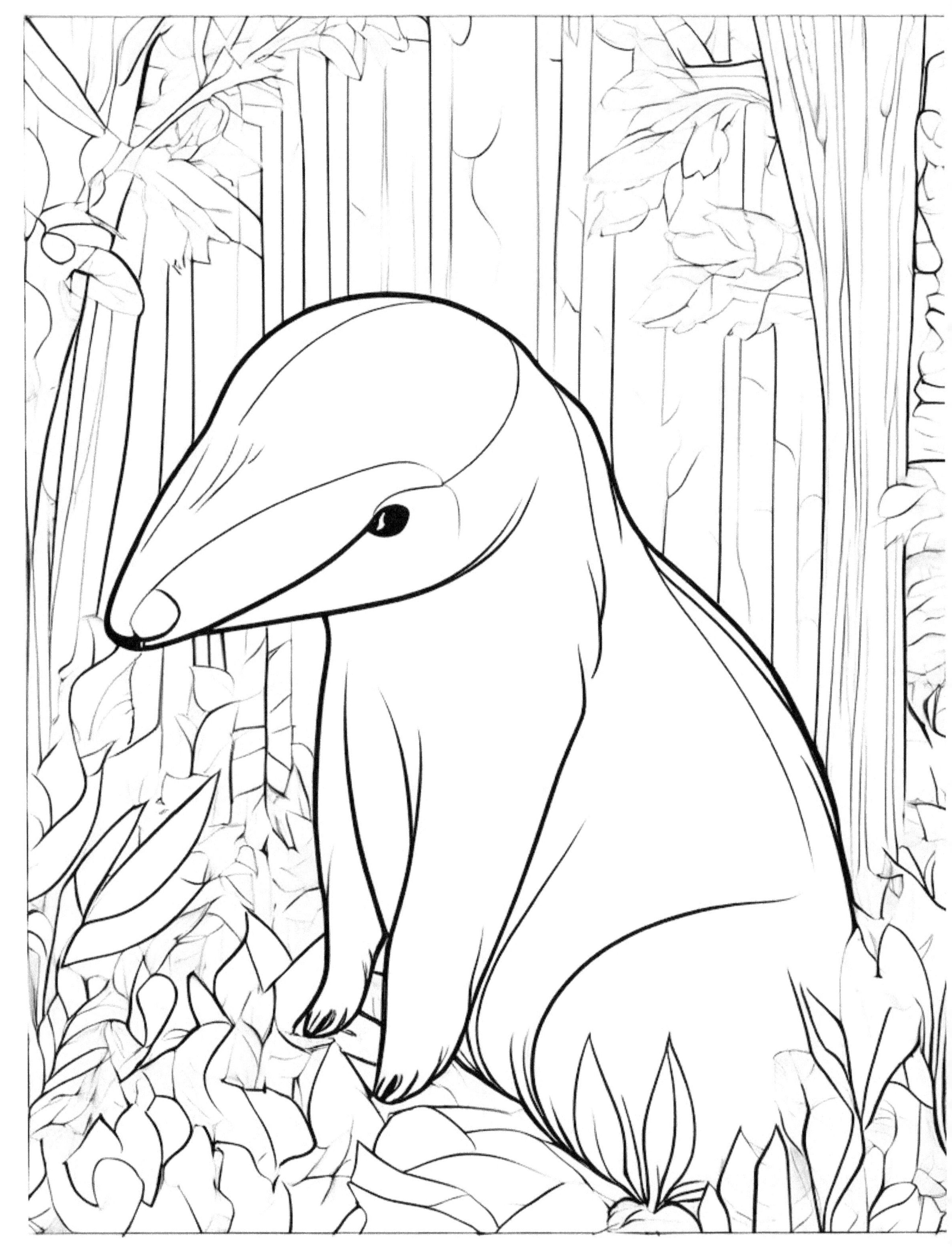

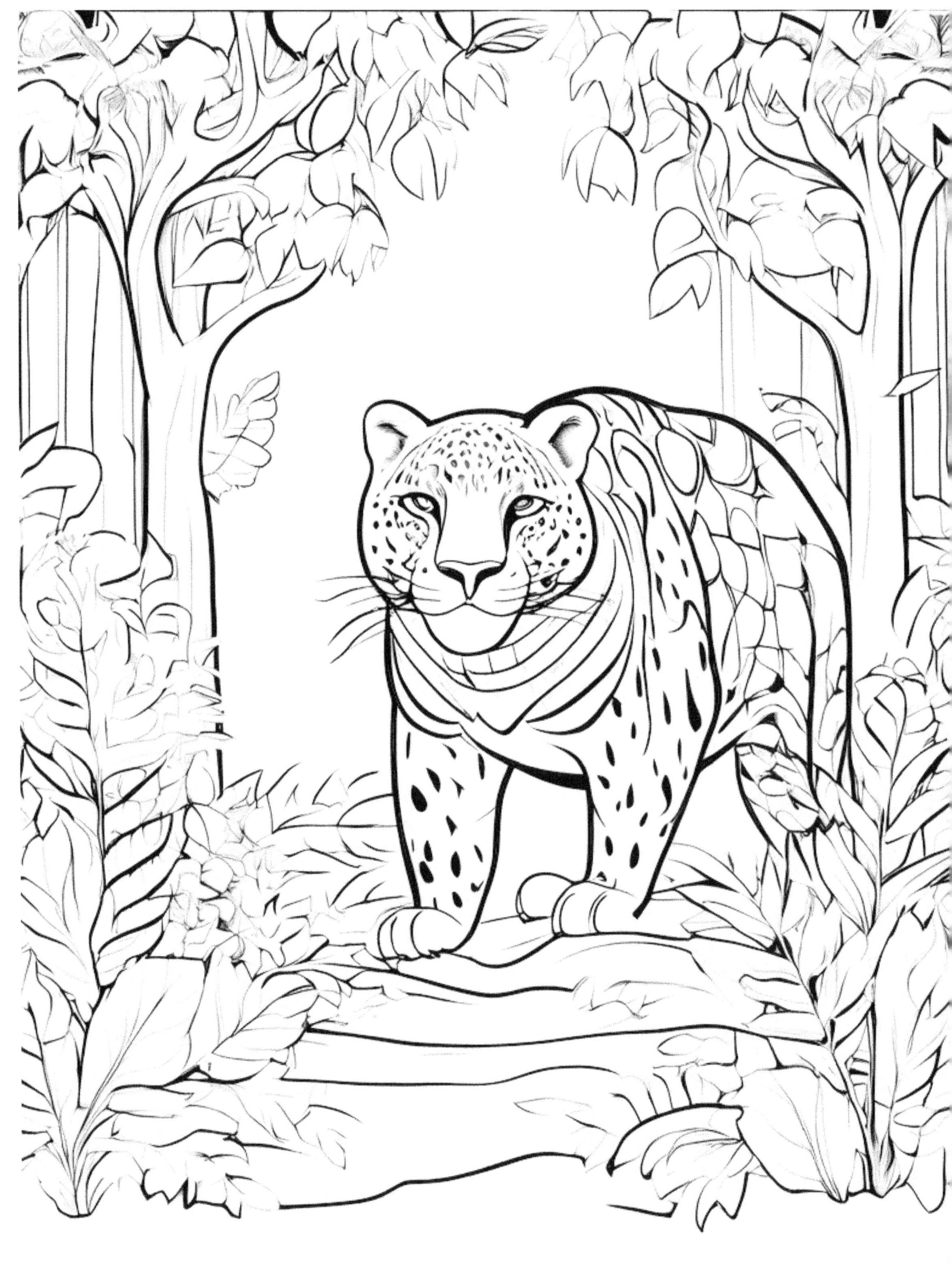

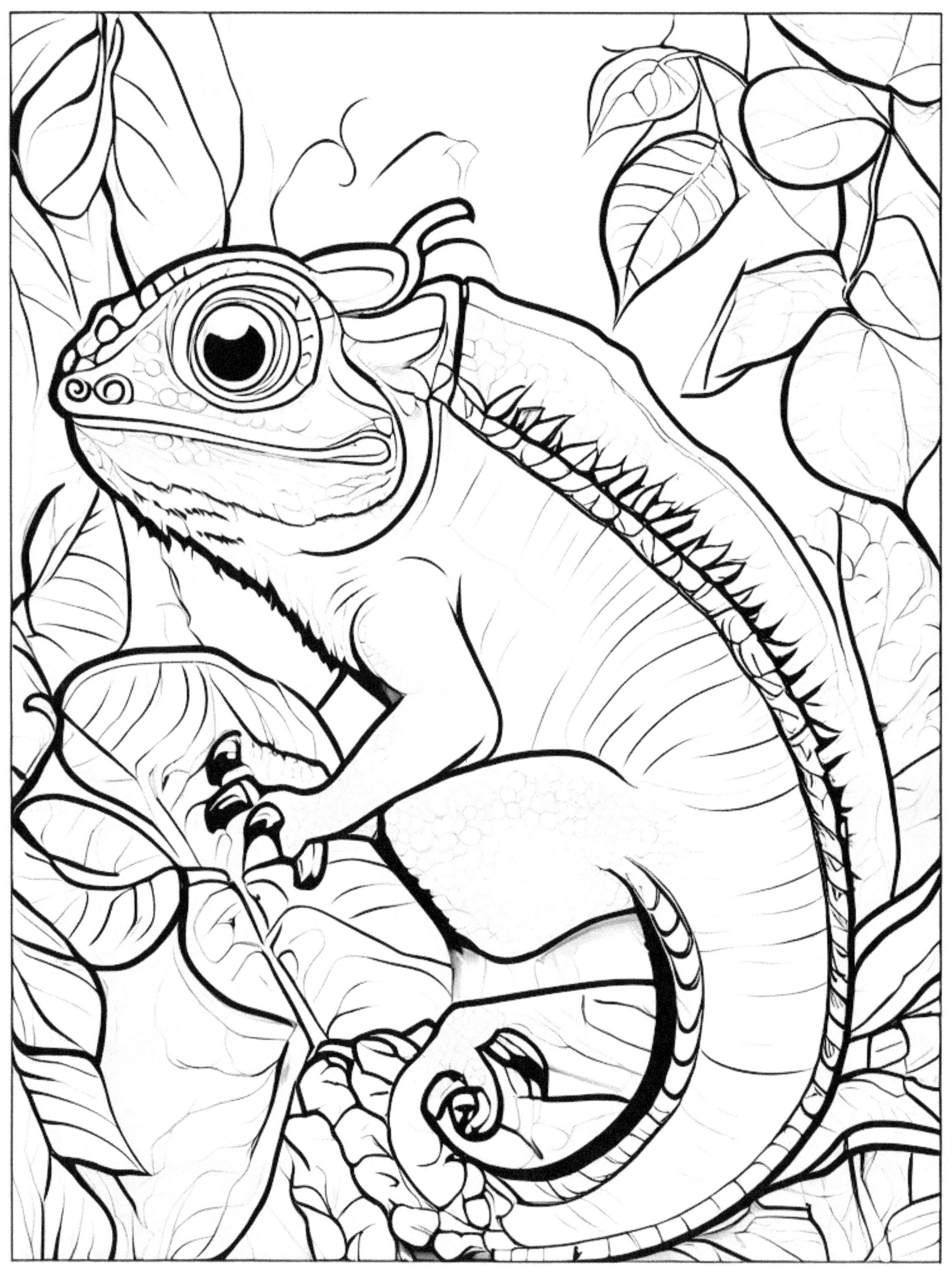

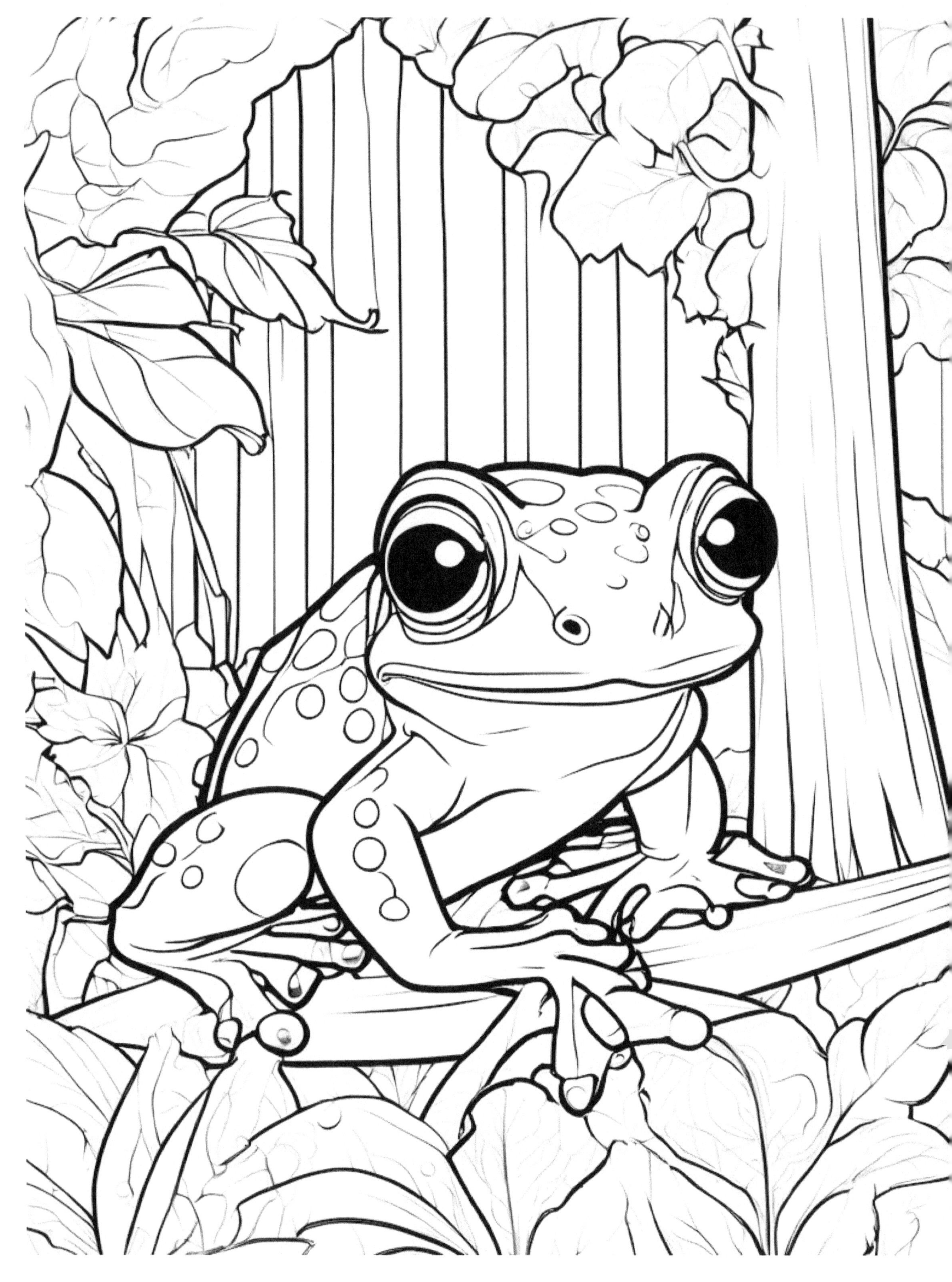

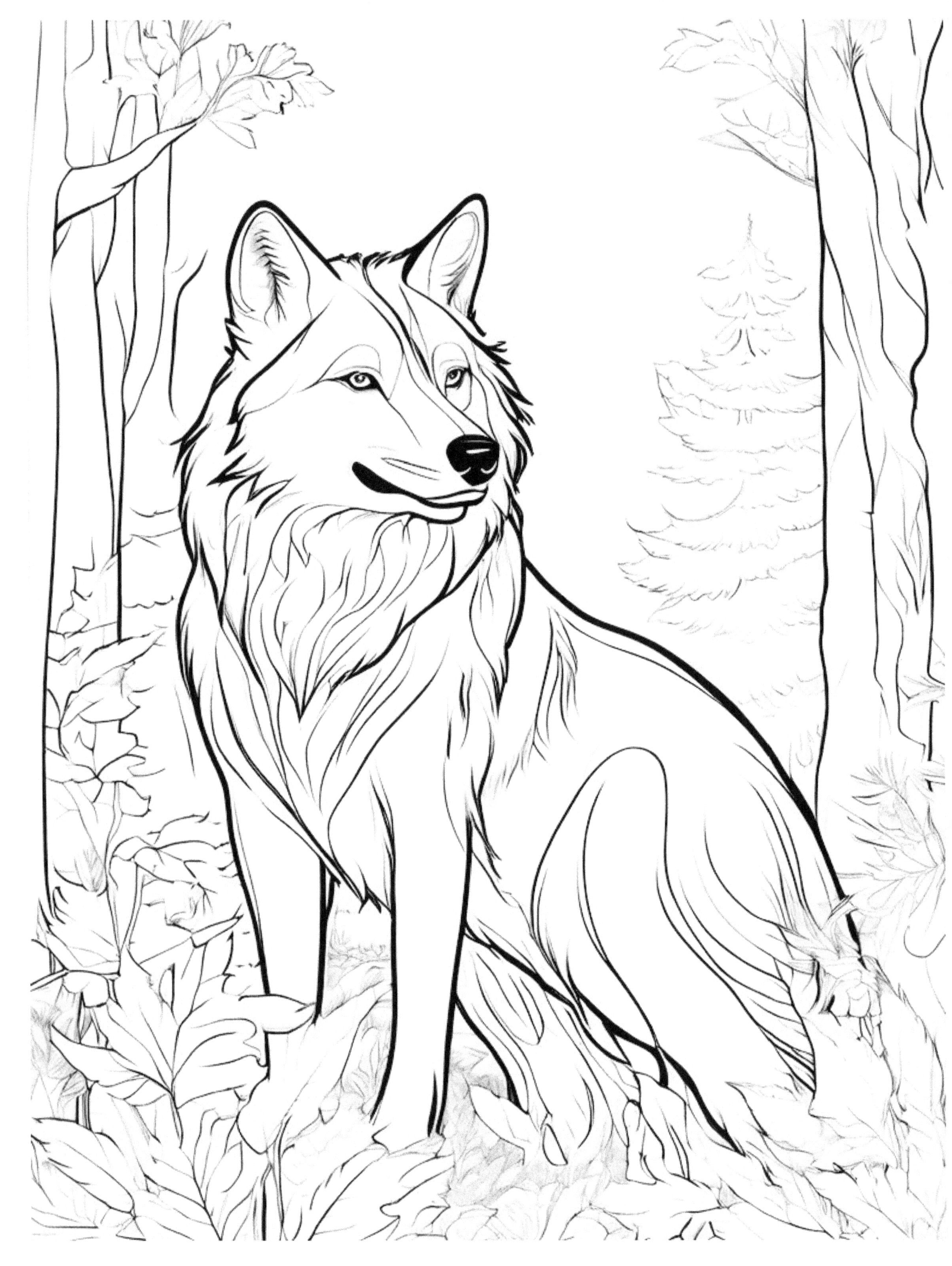

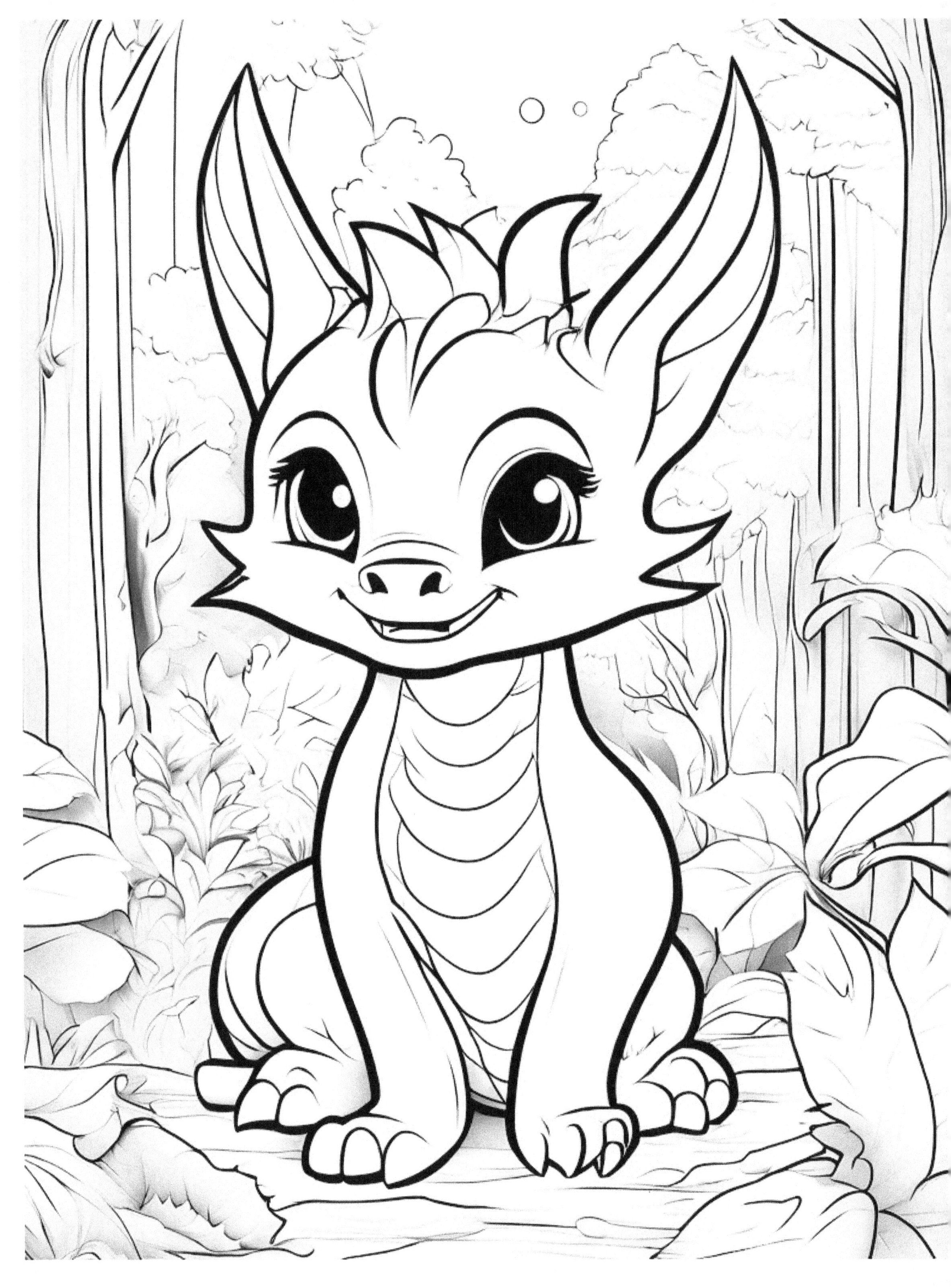

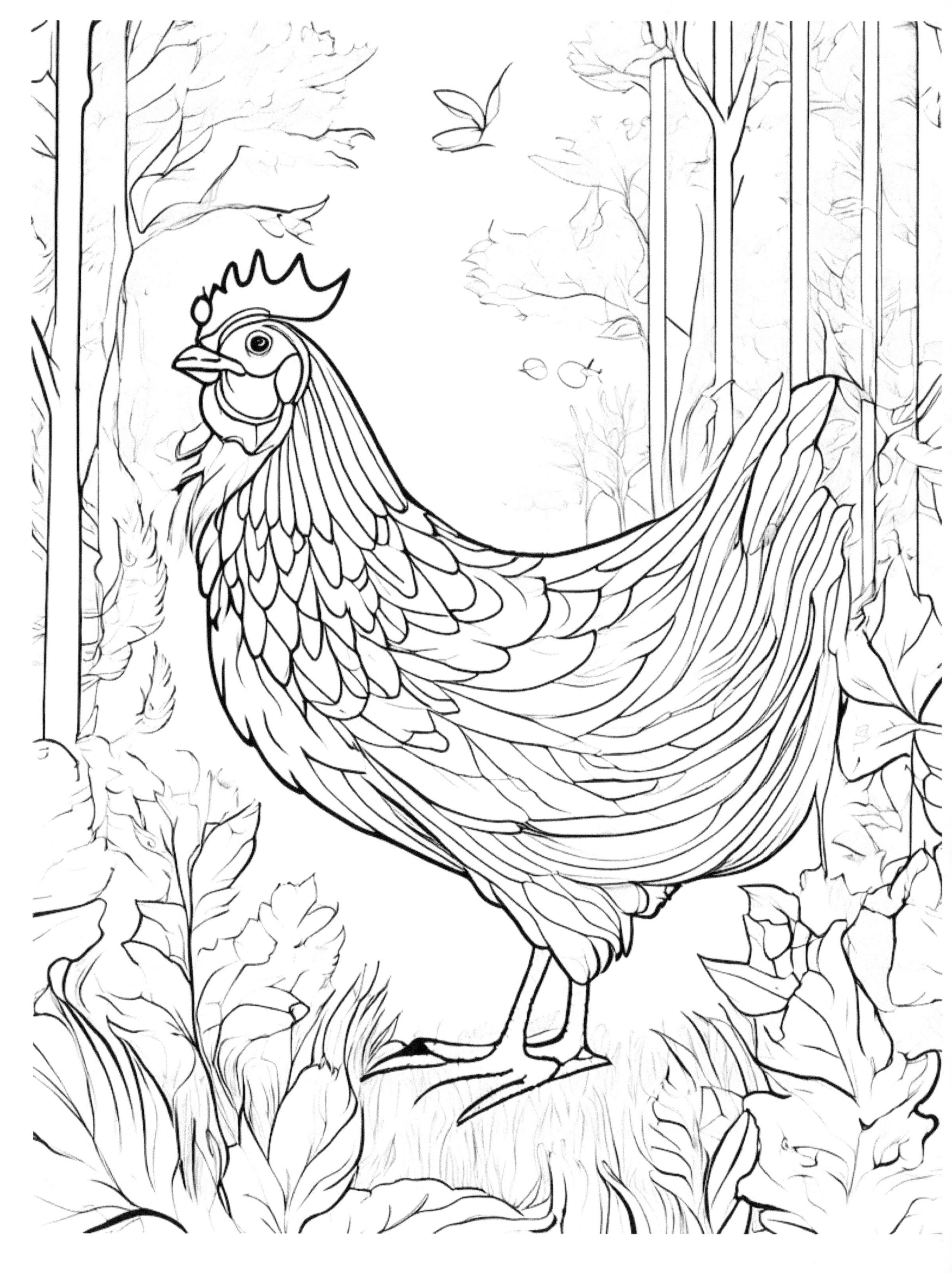

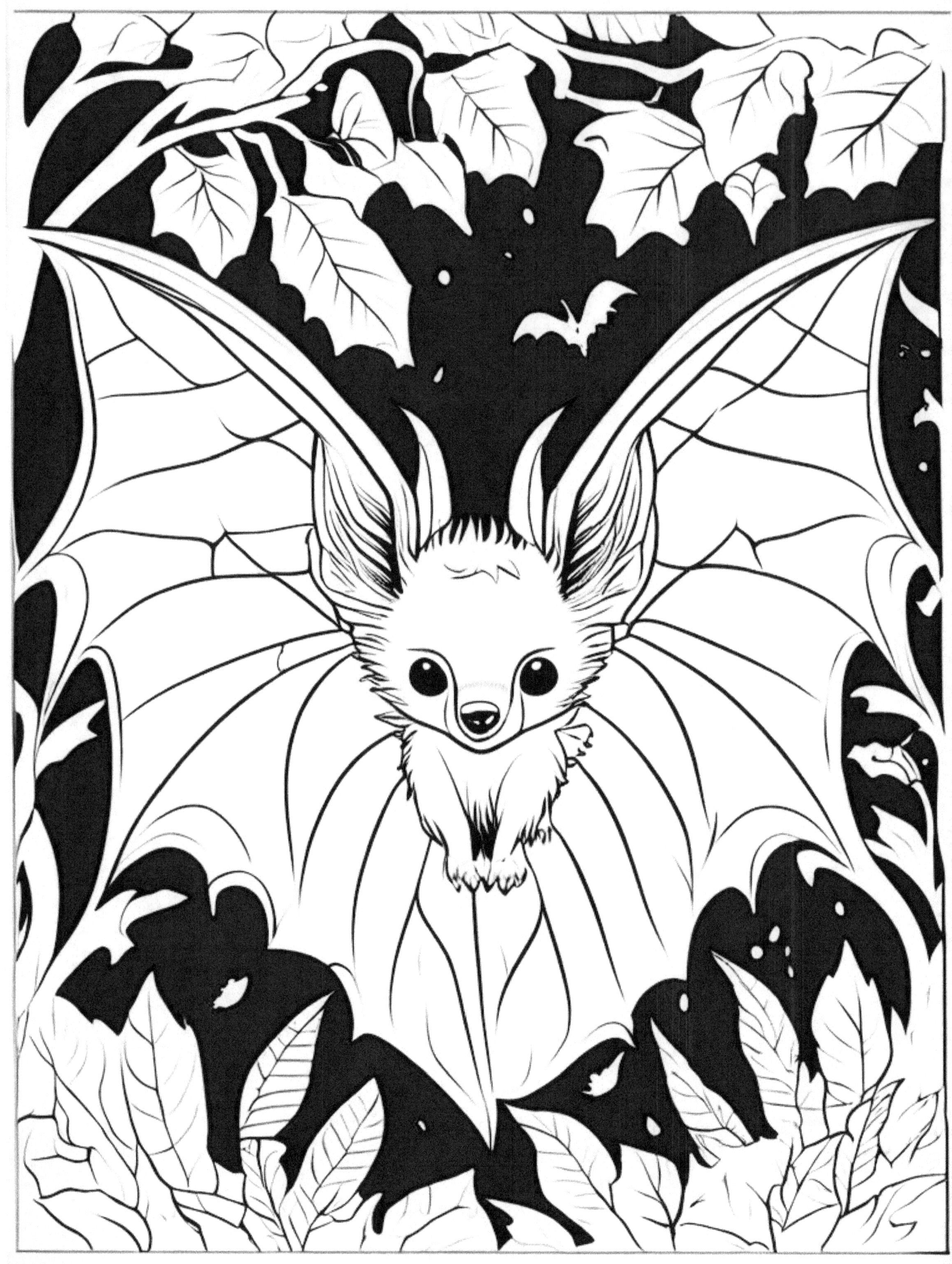

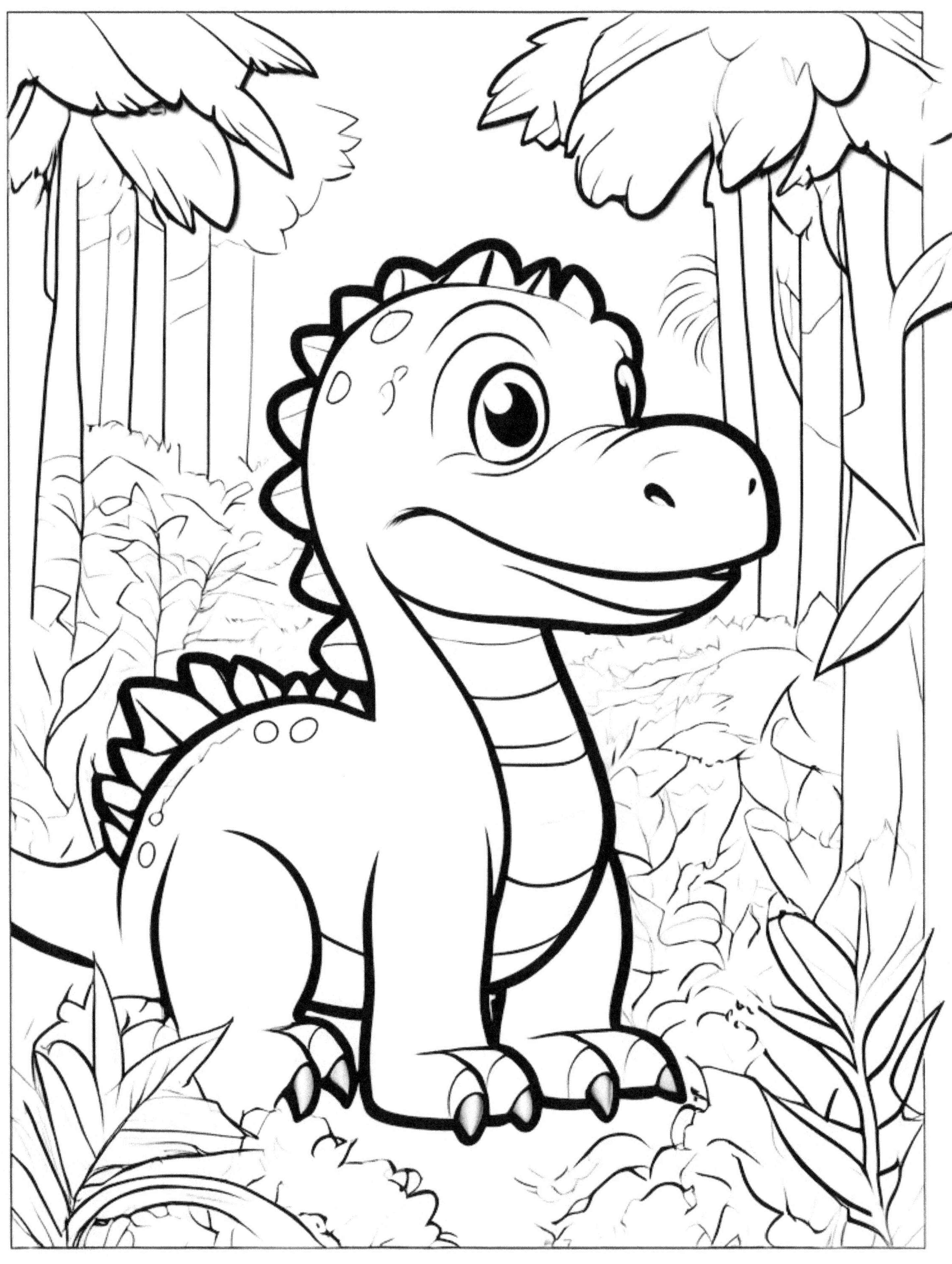

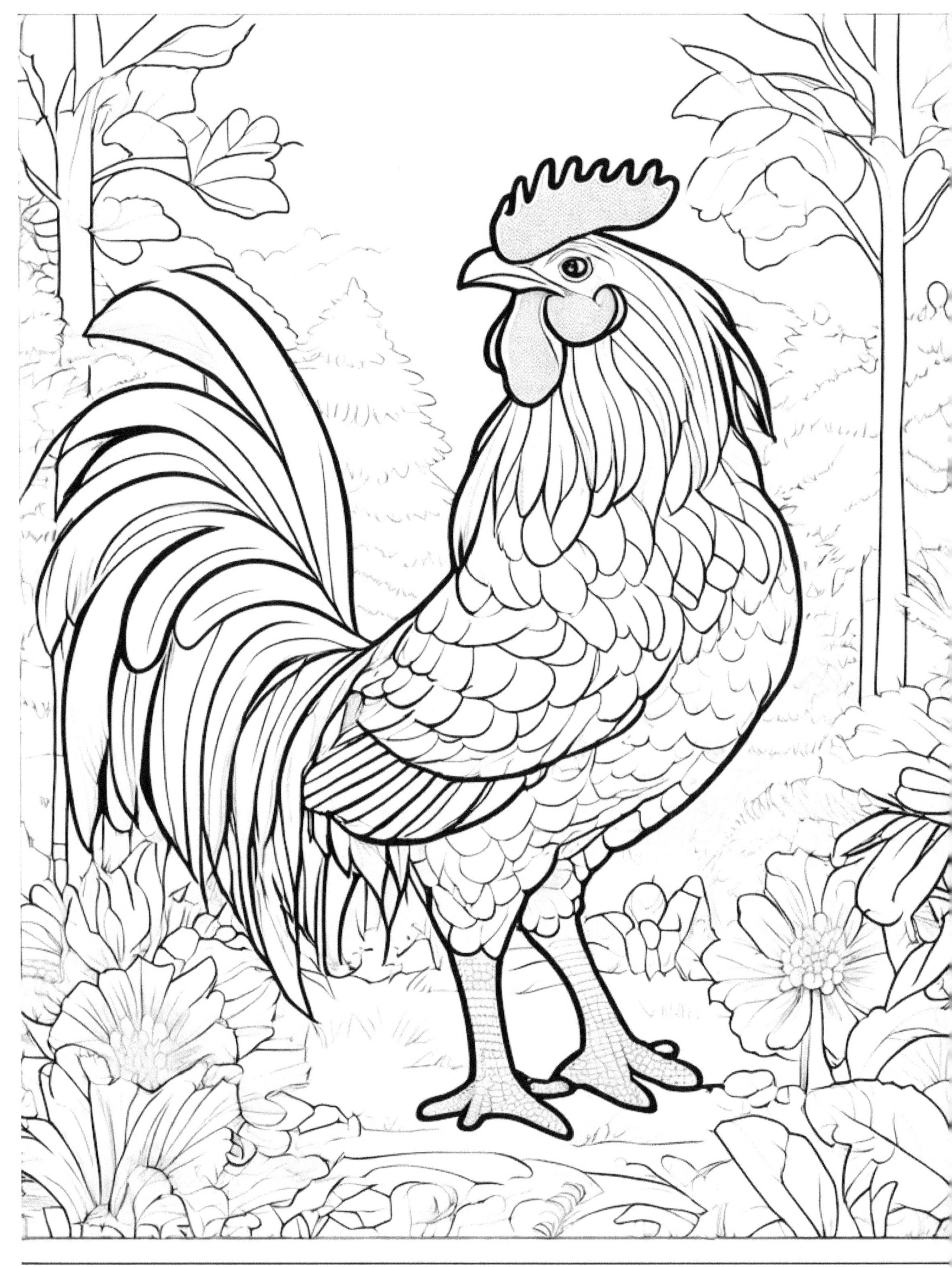

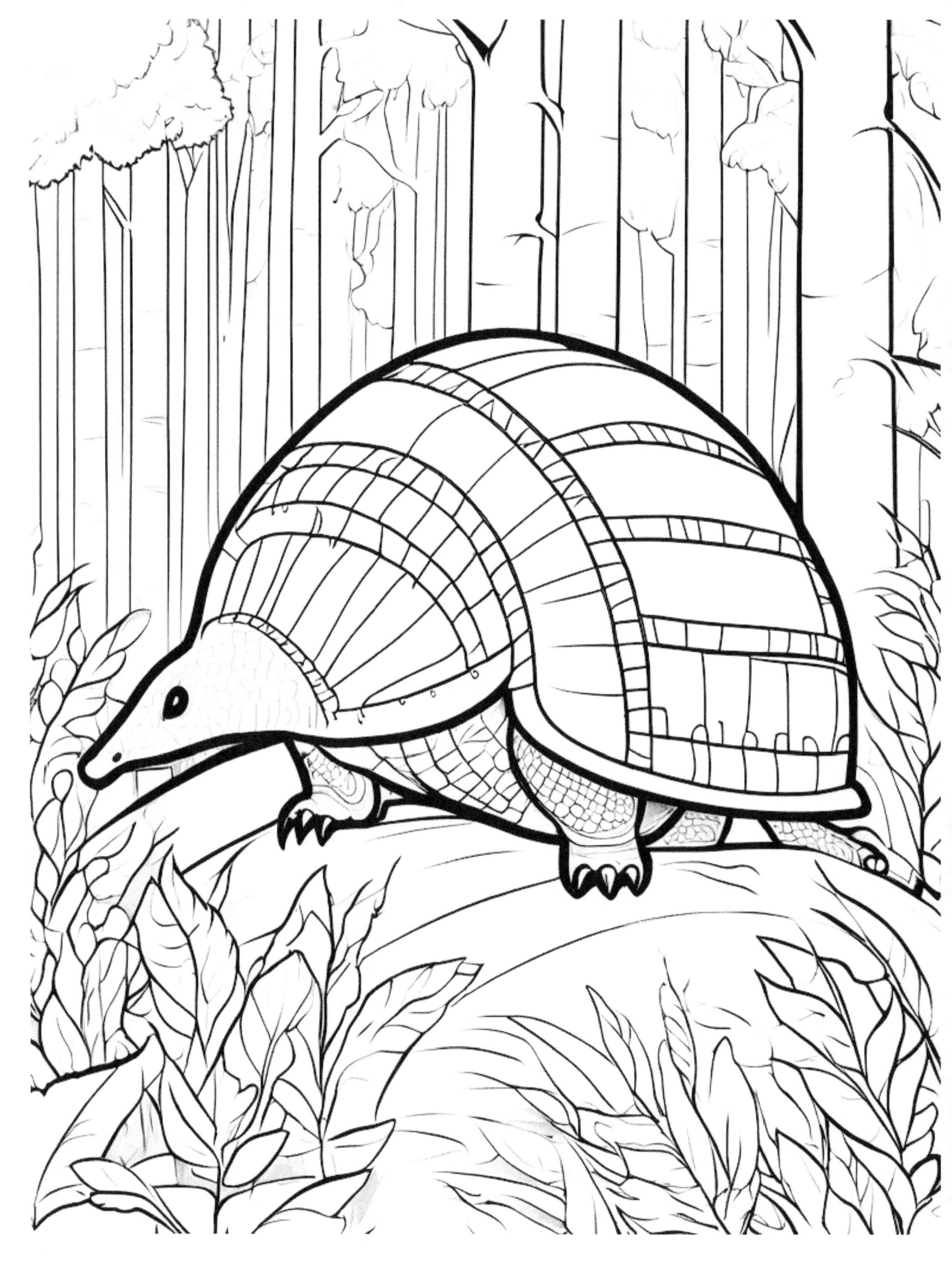

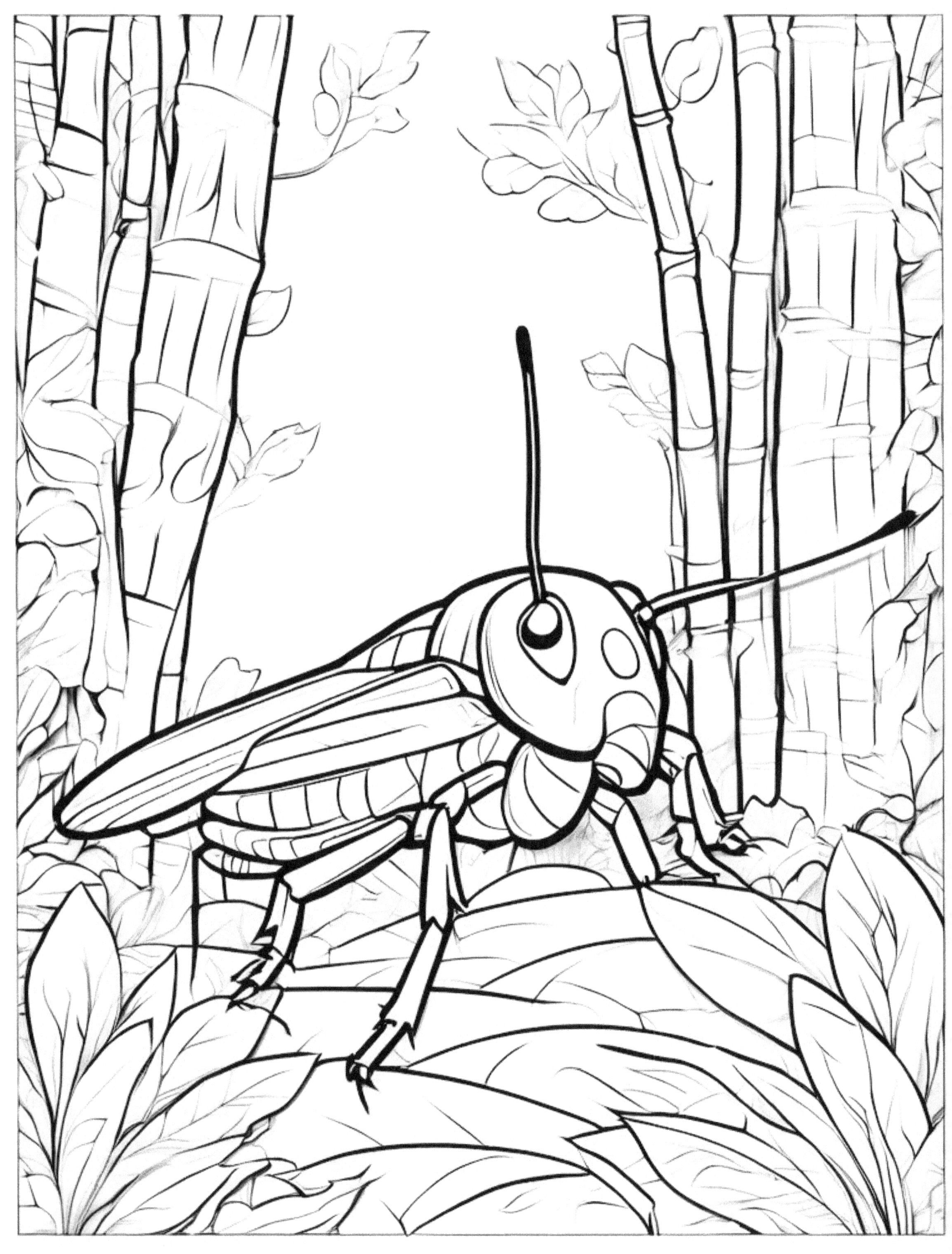

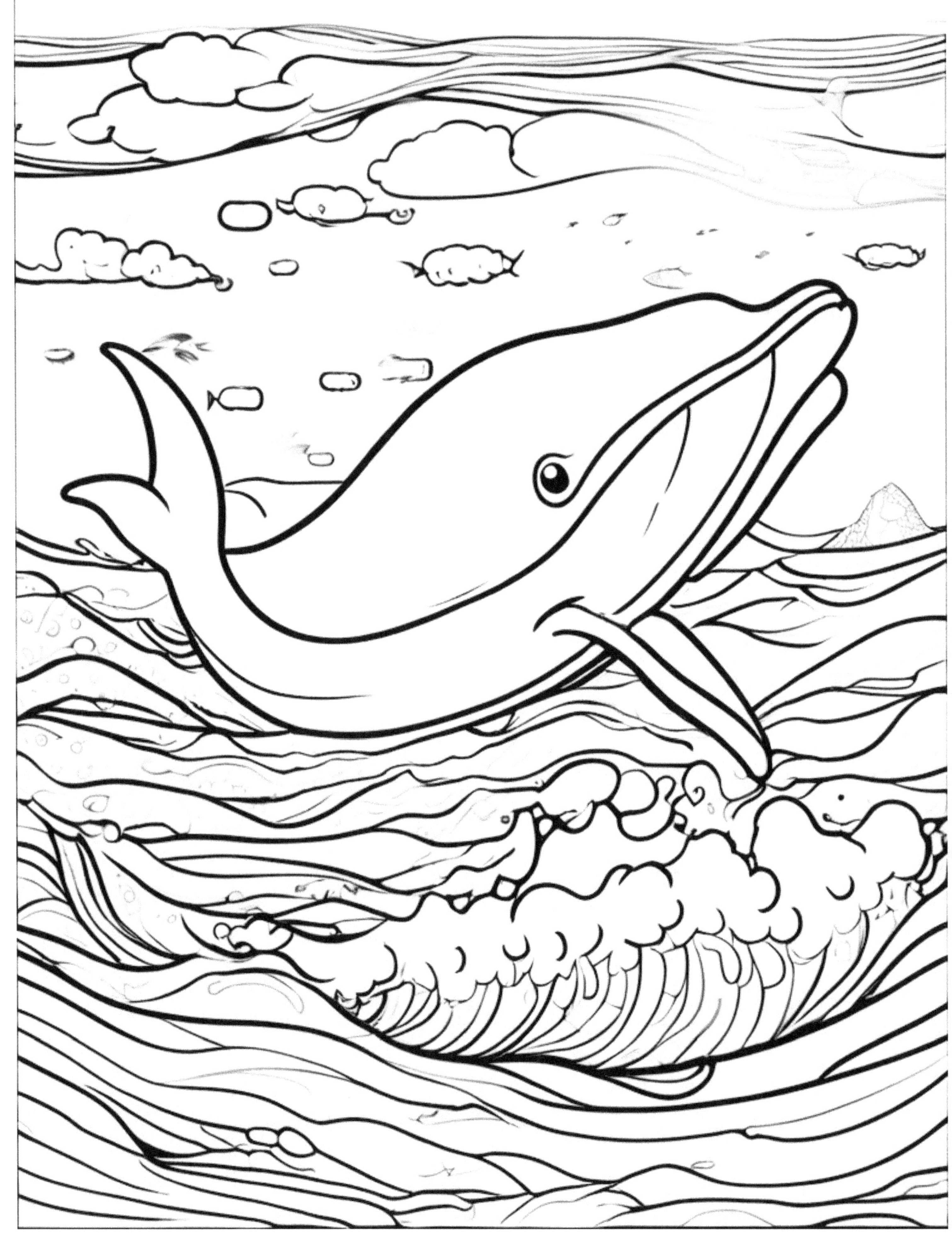

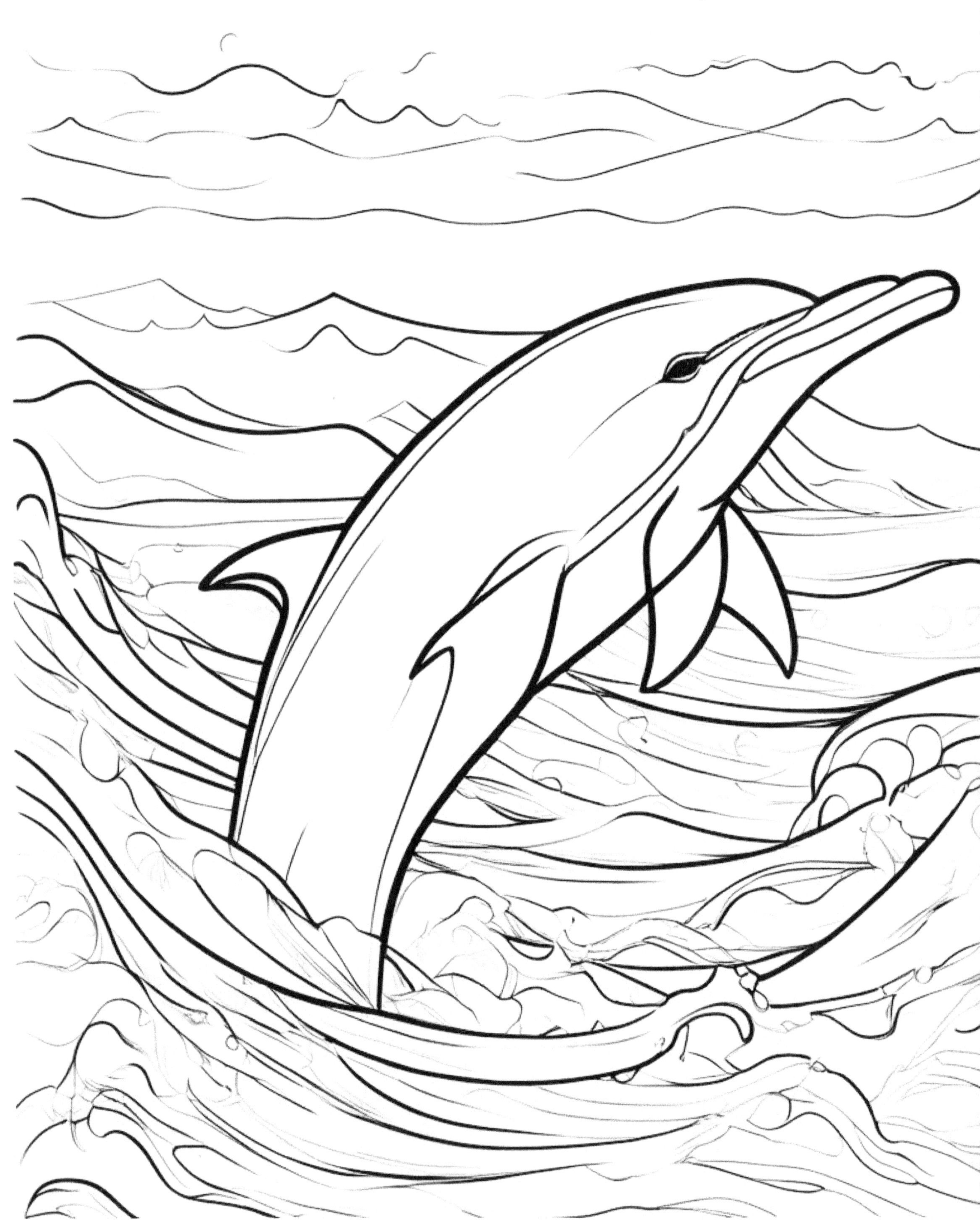

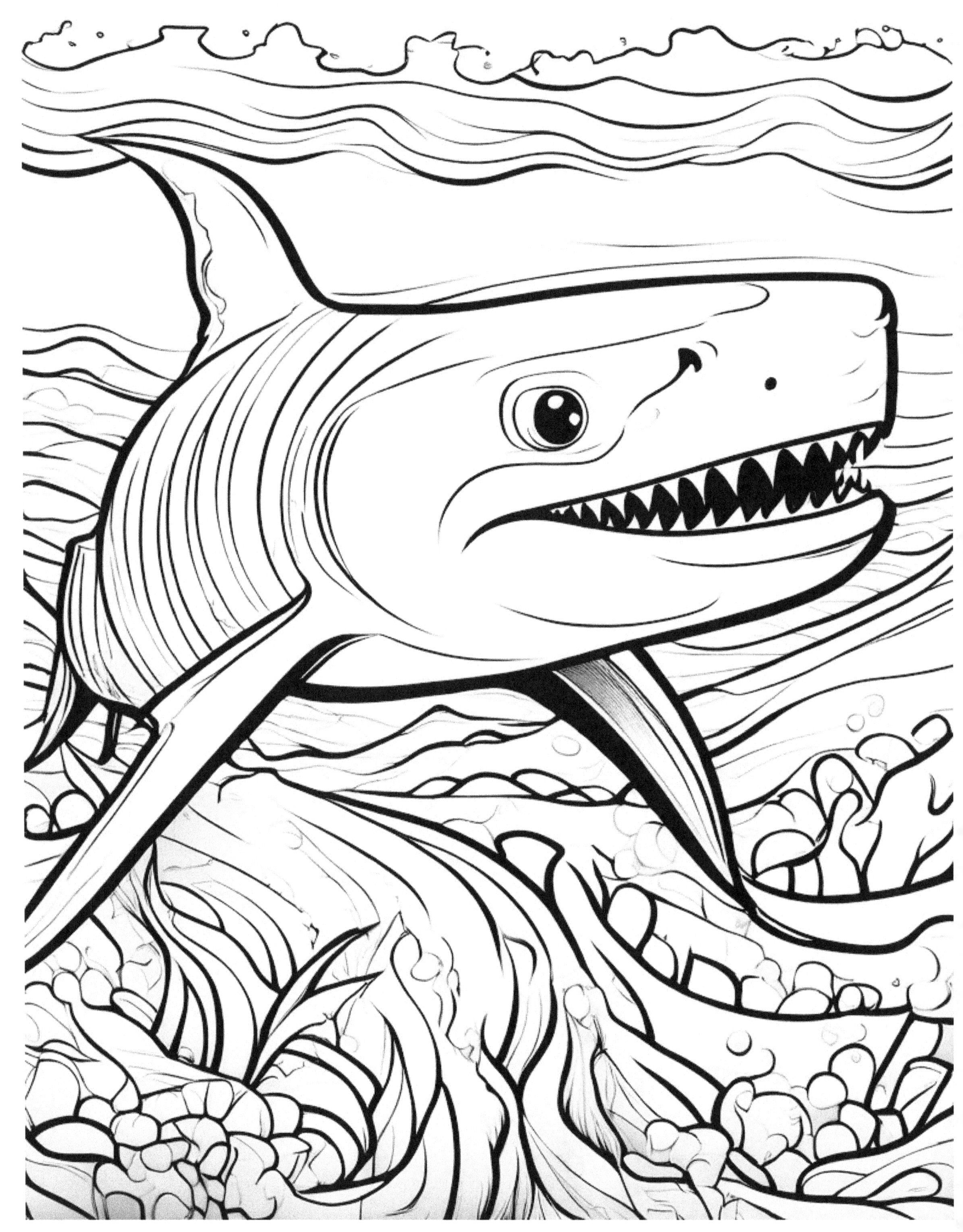

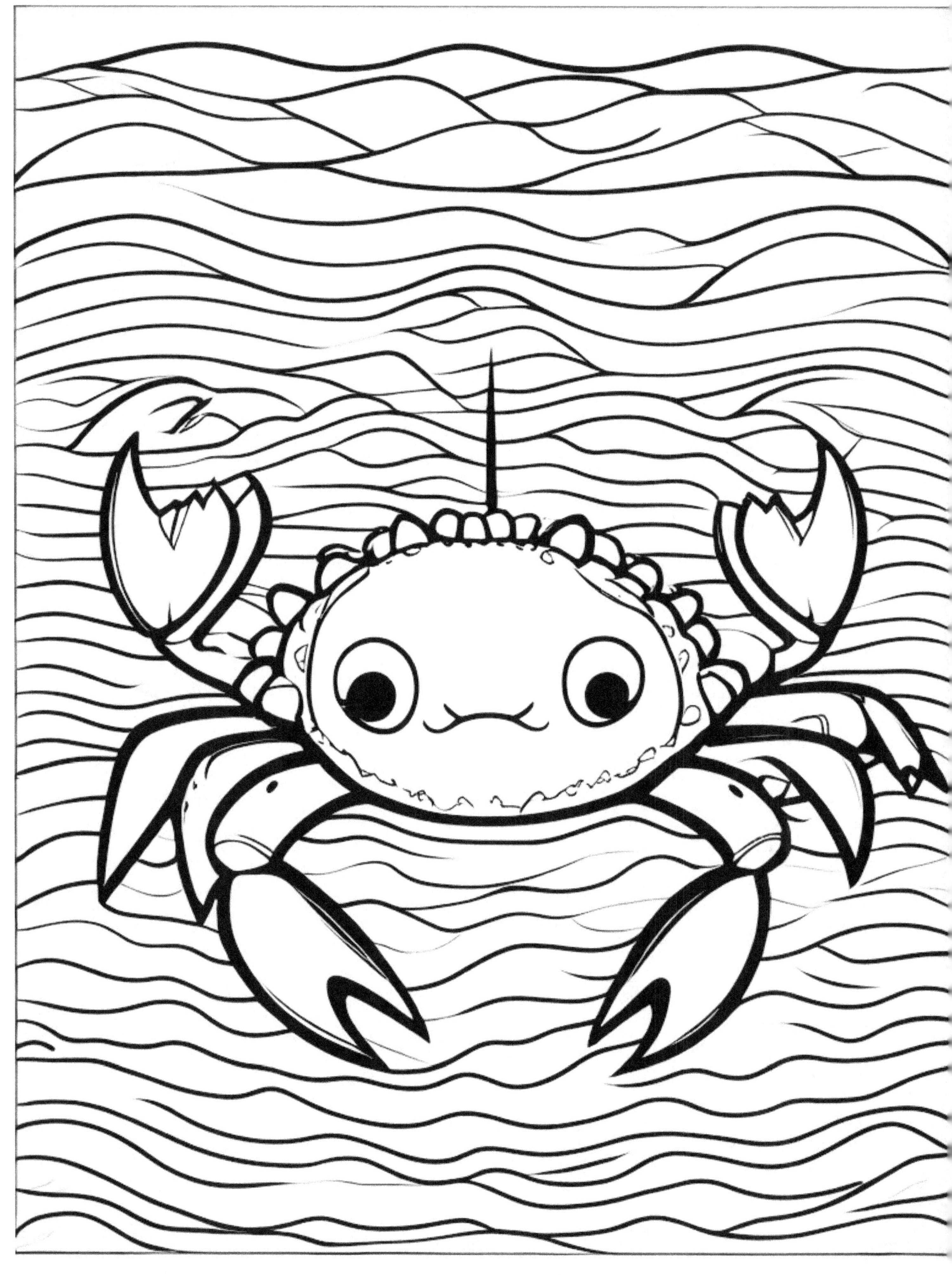

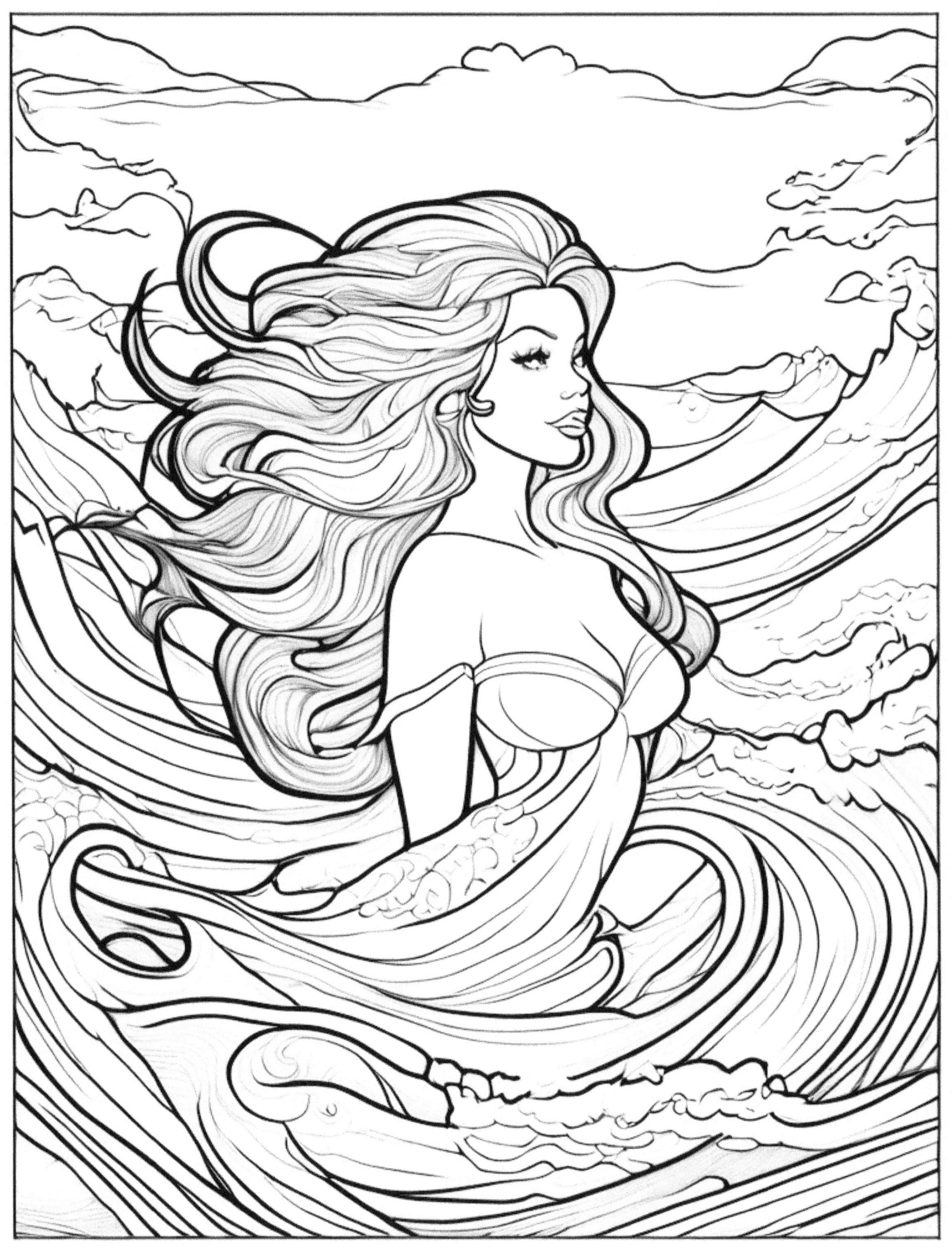